Life Without Stirrups

A Witty Memoir About One Person's Gallop Through Life

Hope you enjoy the book!

Dagny

Dagny Mofid

Copyright © 2015 Dagny Mofid
All rights reserved.

ISBN: 1507624859
ISBN 13: 9781507624852
Library of Congress Control Number: 2015902915
CreateSpace Independent Publishing Platform
North Charleston, South Carolina

To my mother, Helen Eunice Cox Sladeczek

Thank you
For holding my little hands as I took my first steps,
for always encouraging me forward, and
for clapping the loudest when I finally got there.

Table of Contents

Stumbled Beginnings 1

July 8, 1976 12

A Sea Change 27

Lurching Forward 46

La Belle Province 56

Returning to Center 71

In Washington State with No Right Turns 95

In Search of a Male Riding Instructor 117

Time Was Ticking 131

Buying the Evil Demon 148

Young Wine Can Be Sour 159

A Fence Comes Down 177

A Bag Full of Hope 198

Commander of the Armies of the North 220

An Ornamental Disaster 238

Saying Adieu 254

A Band of Gypsies 262

The Golden State and the Golden Horse 276

Finding My Stirrups in a Desert Wash 295

1

Stumbled Beginnings

I could have taken up gardening. It would have been so much easier—no chances of being injured by a giant rhododendron. A late frost would have been my greatest worry and weeds my only real chronic problem. Yes, I could have settled for the gloriously peaceful and neighbor-pleasing art of gardening. By now, most certainly, I would have achieved the pinnacle of success and been named a master gardener; ladies at garden clubs would flock around me, seeking tidbits of wisdom about how to rid their roses of black spot or keep their tomatoes from succumbing to blight. Master gardener—what a wonderful term! I've always wanted to be a master of something. Of course, to have had success early as a child prodigy would have been sweet. What could be better than playing piano concertos to theaters packed full of admiring adults? I would have handled fame well—graciously praising all who had contributed to my success—and never stumbling on my red-velvet gowns.

Sadly, my thirteen-hour birth in the west end of Montreal (albeit tiring for my parents) was as normal as a seed sprouting. The fact that I was born stone-deaf, I admit, was a little odd. Luckily, my dainty ears realized they had a job to do, and hearing mysteriously appeared at the age of five months. Like all good parents, mine were determined to provide their darling daughter—their thankfully no-longer-deaf child—with every reasonable opportunity for success. Yes, under the warm rays of their encouragement, my talents would unfold like a butterfly's wings.

Inspired by what seemed like rhythmical splashing in the bathtub, my parents enrolled me in piano lessons at the tender age of six. After listening for nearly a year to what could only be described as thunderous cries from an underworld, it was with great sadness that my parents broke the news that piano lessons were suddenly and inexplicably no longer available within a fifty-mile radius of our home. As a consolation, I was then gently and enthusiastically herded into art classes for little Monets. Unfortunately, Madame Rousseau, the art teacher, grew increasingly concerned that my heartfelt renditions of impressively large black apples, black cats, thick black grass, and black clouds held demonic meaning. She suggested, with utmost seriousness, that my energies should be channeled elsewhere before a stabbing ensued.

Shaken, but not defeated, my parents quickly aborted my career in fine art, and, despite considerable protest on my part, I was enrolled in the local girls' soccer team. Apparently, my stocky legs had not gone unnoticed. When the coach realized I could not run fast and had no stamina, I was placed in the all-too-important position of goalie. Unfortunately for my teammates, I had no desire to stop the ball—believing that the white-and-black spinning missile was better avoided than tackled. Somewhat disappointed, my parents set their sights on my academic career. Yes, one night after a particularly deep discussion of the subtle nuances of my character, they decided it had been an error to assume that my talents lay in sports, music, or art—for it was in the classroom that the greatest minds flourished. Like them, I would appreciate philosophy and the classics of literature, and I'd certainly excel at math and science. When I proudly presented my report card that year, which I thought featured a pretty consistent list of C-minuses, they did seem oddly quiet.

Luckily, it was at this same time that horses mysteriously trotted themselves into my young soul. The idea of Equus—a magical creature that could run like the wind and carve the air with its flowing mane and tail—had first grabbed hold of my imagination years earlier in the backseat of our yellow Volkswagen beetle. Mother had started it all. Yes, mothers can always be blamed. With the same excitement one would normally reserve for a chance meeting with the queen, Mother would cry out her praises for every horse we drove past: "Dagny, did you see the horse? Look at the beautiful horsey! Oh, that one was magnificent! Did you see the star on his forehead? Oh, and the foal! The foal! Did you see that precious foal with its mother?"

It didn't really seem to matter to her that my child-safe seatbelt made peering out of our Volkswagen's window and actually seeing the magical creatures impossible. So as not to disappoint, I would always confirm the sighting with dutiful nods and a "Yes, Mommy, I saw them," even if all I had really seen were treetops and a few feisty black crows.

I wonder if Mother suspected her own love of horses would result in her daughter taking up one of the most expensive hobbies on the planet. Given our rather humble means, perhaps she should have pointed out every bird she saw instead. Birding would have been a much less expensive and safer pastime. Even peregrine falcons don't take aim at the khaki-covered birders peering quietly at them from the underbrush.

At the age of eight, with my little-league soccer career but a distant memory, I asked Mother if I could have horseback riding lessons. Pleased as pink that her daughter had finally demonstrated an interest in something, *Oh please, God, anything*, I was quickly enrolled in weekend riding camps at the Covey Hill Horse Center—a riding school for girls about forty rolling miles south of the city of Montreal. Once a month, Mother would selflessly drive the eighty-mile round trip (she assured me), so her darling daughter could have the finest riding instruction available. Terrible snowstorms did not seem to weaken her determination to drop me off promptly at 7:00 p.m., Friday evenings. In parallel, and with suspiciously similar timing, my father whisked my brother off to hockey camp. It is still unclear to me how my parents suffered through those child-free weekends.

The Covey Hill Horse Center, it turned out, was modeled with German precision and Amish austerity. The farm itself was perched atop a large hill surrounded by a tightly knit forest of maple and fir trees. A great swath of trees had been meticulously cleared to make way for the large, gray A-frame barn and its matching gabled farmhouse. The buildings featured clean lines, lacked any form of decoration, and exuded strength of purpose. The heavy doors, thick-plastered white walls, and roughhewn ceiling beams seemed quite capable of tackling even our worst Canadian winter.

The stable was a rectangular, center-aisle barn with attached indoor arena. The arena was enormous and its roof sharply peaked to encourage snow to glide off in the wintertime. The barn was home to twenty horses. Ten horses enjoyed roomy, square stalls while the other ten had to make do with narrow, standing stalls. I'm not quite sure why the real estate had been unfairly divided, but I assumed, given the hayloft, that the horses had drawn straws. Just to the left of the barn was a meticulously graded outdoor riding ring. Fine gravel had been laid down around the base of each building, and any shrub, flower, or dandelion that dared to come within two hundred feet of any foundation was uprooted without sympathy. Fire safety, we were told, was an important factor in horse-barn management.

Horse-crazy girls that had signed up for the Center's "weekend intensives" were housed in the left wing of the farmhouse. Our meals were served communal style on solid wooden tables carefully protected with plastic-laminated tablecloths. I had never seen tablecloths made of plastic before—these were bright-red plaid. I couldn't decide if the owners were trying to give the room a country feel or a pizzeria look. We were handed our meal plates via a wooden half door that divided the eating area from the kitchen. The owners said the half door was there to keep the shepherd dogs out of the kitchen. After observing how obedient the dogs were, I concluded the half door was really to keep us kids out of what appeared to be the better part of the house.

At the corner of our country "dining room" was a narrow, curving staircase that shot steeply up into an attic that had been converted into a dormitory. Truth be told, the room had all the appeal of a World War II orphanage. It was a narrow, rectangular room outfitted with military-style bunk beds that could accommodate sixteen girls. The plywood walls had been painted with a thick coat of white, and our only view was through two uncurtained, gabled windows that looked out over the steel-gray gravel parking lot. I couldn't figure out why the windows were nailed shut. Perhaps a child had tried to escape one night? More likely, the owners didn't want us children adjusting the room's temperature.

My first night at Covey Hill was a restless one. I was terribly excited about my riding lessons and not used to the sounds of other girls tossing in their beds. As I lay there thinking, I suddenly realized that the narrow, twirling staircase was our only exit out of the room. Thank goodness for those fire-safety measures.

I soon realized that each weekend's schedule of activities had been given considerable thought and never varied. Students were fed breakfast, lunch, and dinner at set times. We were given two riding lessons on Saturday and one on Sunday morning. Saturday mornings began at 6:00 a.m., when we were given the opportunity to hone our horse-care skills. "Mucking stalls," we discovered, was a term that meant shoveling horse poop into wobbly old wheelbarrows and hauling it off to a manure pile that seemed inconveniently placed far from the barn. "Horse care" involved washing buckets and horse brushes, removing cobwebs from stalls, and sweeping the barn aisles morning, noon, and night. We cleaned saddles and bridles with glycerin soap and leather cream and then buffed them shiny with old rags. Students were also asked to help mend fences, wash horse blankets, disinfect incredibly heavy stall mats, and wash the barn bathroom. Of course, this was all done to teach us "responsibility."

Each weekend, we bathed and groomed the school horses to perfection, and the barn owners' personal horses were added to the "to be cleaned" roster for good measure. I wonder if our parents realized the brilliance of this setup. Or maybe they wanted to be rid of us children so much that they didn't mind if we had to do a little weekend slave labor? Each day (once we finished learning a tremendous amount of "responsibility"), we were given how-to lessons on horse care, grooming techniques, horse anatomy, and all matters horse related. Between daily chores, our lectures on horse care, and our actual riding lessons, we were kept busy from the moment we woke up to the moment we fell back onto those thinly blanketed bunk beds and desperately tried to pull our sore, blistered feet out of the boots we had worn all day.

Interestingly enough, the instructors at Covey Hill seemed intent on returning horsemanship to its military roots. The first rule of riding, we were told, was that any student who fell off, had not lost consciousness, and was not bleeding profusely must immediately remount. To prepare for the inevitable, the instructors would have us trot around the ring en masse, and at their command "Dismount!" all the students had to propel themselves off of their mounts, attempt to land on their feet, and then immediately roll and bounce back up again.

I was initially deeply suspicious of this teaching technique and wondered if our parents were aware of the acrobatic component of the curriculum. However, as time went on, there seemed to be some wisdom in the practice. Horses, I discovered, can execute abrupt full stops and make sharp, unexpected turns right or left without even a polite word of warning to their riders. My personal fall rate per class hovered around 50 percent. In fact, as the months went on, I sometimes wondered if the instructors took bets on whether I would fall off during a lesson or not. I fell into fences and into walls—most often over the top of the horse's head—or slid ungraciously down around its midsection. Sometimes I would lose my balance and end up hanging from the horse's neck as it trotted around the ring, not quite knowing when the best time to let go was. It was my good fortune that horses don't particularly like to step on unusual objects, and each time I fell, they graciously sidestepped my limbs as they sauntered away with glee. For the horses, ditching their riders seemed the highlight of their day. Each time I fell, the instructors—apparently having quickly surmised I hadn't died and determined not to delay the lesson—would yell, "Mount up!" Considering all the bruises I hid from my mother, there is some benefit to starting to ride when you are young and flexible and can bounce back from injury.

Even though our lessons were group lessons of five or six riders per class, the instructors were terribly fair and shouted at each of us. I can still hear the instructor's voice as she tried to convey to me the time-honored English riding position. "Dagny, keep your heels down. Dagny, look ahead, eyes straight ahead. No, sit up straight. Straighter than that! Remember, *heels down*. Now, ask for a trot. Eyes up, check your diagonal, walk...and halt. Halt, Dagny. Yes, now, halt, halt... OK, return to center."

About four months after I started attending these weekend boot camps at Covey Hill, Quebec winter set in, and I slowly became aware that my attire was totally unsuited to riding in an unheated barn at minus four degrees Fahrenheit. Now, in addition to worrying about whether I was posting the trot on the correct diagonal, I began to worry whether I would lose a toe to frostbite or be able to move my fingers enough to unsaddle my mount. Not wanting to put any additional financial burden on my parents, I felt compelled to tell them that my cotton socks and rubber rain boots were functioning *just fine* as horse attire, and no, those polyester riding gloves were perfect.

To add to the physical challenge of riding with frozen extremities was the embarrassment of knowing I was the worst rider in the group. Even my instructors seemed to want to disassociate themselves from my performance—when my name was called at pony-club horse shows, they would suddenly disappear or become suspiciously preoccupied with picking fluff off of their jackets. You see, everyone in the stands knows it is the horse that is supposed to jump the cavaletti, and the child is not to fly over first.

By the time spring had finally thawed the eastern townships, and despite several ominous-looking bruises on my thighs and backside, horses had become my obsession, and

Covey Hill had become my favorite place in the world. I started to love the smell of hay and leather and learned that, at least on a farm, it was OK to get a little dusty, to have pieces of hay in my hair, and to laugh when a horse sneezed his snot all over me. I have no recollection of ever showering at Covey Hill. I can just imagine how stinky I must have been on Sunday afternoons when Mother picked me up. I'm sure I projected a unique combination of sweat, dirt, and utter contentment.

In truth, my equestrian boot-camp experiences taught me a few important life lessons: some tasks, like catching horses, require patience and a bit of ingenuity; when the last morsel of air seems to have been punched out of your body, the lungs know just what to do; when your face turns beet red, it doesn't last forever; a friend can really help when you're trying to pull a boot off; white is not a color you should wear to a barn; cats really can catch mice; and horses are incredibly beautiful, strong, patient, forgiving, smart, high-maintenance creatures. Unfortunately, just as I began to enjoy the idea that I was "a horseback rider"—proudly telling the girls at school all about my "horsey" weekends—life threw me a curve ball. Actually, no—in truth, life threw a mallet.

2

July 8, 1976

Any day can change your life. I have no recollection of that fateful morning. My remembering starts only at around four in the afternoon. My father and I were sitting on bleachers at Parc Rabastalière, watching my brother, Earl, play soccer. It was unusually hot that afternoon, and since it was a Thursday, there were only a few parents in the stands. Dad was watching the two teams of twelve- and thirteen-year-old boys charge back and forth across the field, clenching his knees in anticipation every time Earl took control of the ball and began racing with it toward the opponent's goal. My father, a German immigrant to Canada, loved soccer as most Europeans do. Dad had played the game constantly when he was a boy, and he had the thick, soccer-seasoned legs to prove it. My father was not a tall man and somewhat stocky of build, but most thought him handsome, as he had dark black hair; shockingly deep-blue eyes; a well-chiseled face; and a strong, deeply cleft chin.

Although he coached little-league soccer, Dad never coached my brother's team, preferring to cheer him on from the sidelines. I still didn't grasp the rules of the game, but my brother seemed to possess a competitive spirit, often stealing the ball away from boys bigger than him and scoring whenever he spotted a sliver of opportunity. Although he was small in stature, with thin, little legs, Earl had the lungs and speed of a caribou. Having spent the spring and summer outdoors, his skin was already deeply tanned and this, combined with his brown hair and deep-blue eyes, made him look more like a young Italian boy than your average pasty-white Canadian. Oddly enough, the team's uniform was a horizontally striped yellow-and-black shirt with matching yellow shorts, making the boys appear like a swarm of bees on the field.

Unfortunately, both of my parents were somewhat delusional and carried around the ridiculous hope that their two children truly liked one another. They believed, naïvely, that Earl valued my presence at his soccer game and that I, his younger sister, wanted to applaud his achievements. Little did they remember that just the week before, he had painted mustaches on all my teddy bears and changed the channel from my cherished *Bonanza* to *Star Trek*. No, as he was my mortal enemy, more evil than any Klingon, I was determined to maintain the chasm between us and deliberately tried to avoid looking at the field.

Bored to tears, I occupied myself by trying to visually locate a cicada buzzing in an adjacent tree. One wouldn't think that the small town of Saint Bruno, Quebec, known for its long, cold winters and great cross-country skiing, could experience hot, cicada-buzzing summer days. The mysterious cicada had always fascinated me. Like the Holy Ghost described at Catholic mass, one was to believe in its existence even if it couldn't be seen. The creature's buzzing always started low and soft but quickly crescendoed like a wind-up toy to pneumatic speed. At its fever pitch, I truly expected the animal would self-destruct and reveal its location, but the buzzing would suddenly come to an abrupt, full stop. I would then send my eyes traveling along another branch, hoping against hope I would catch a glimpse of this well-camouflaged insect.

Dad eventually noticed I wasn't watching the players and said, "Dagny, you can go home if you're bored."

"Really?" I replied with glee and a smile. "You don't mind?"

"No, I don't mind. Tell your mother we'll be home by seven o'clock for dinner."

LIFE WITHOUT STIRRUPS

Freed from the task of watching the game, I gingerly made my way down the bleachers, jumping the alternate rows until I reached the grass. Grabbing my pink-ribboned bike, which leaned against the bottom step, I mounted up and proceeded to ride away. Just as I was leaving, I turned back to wave goodbye to my father. Stupidly pedaling forward while looking backward at him, it was only moments later that I crashed wheel first into the chain link fence separating the bleachers from the field. Dad ran down to help me up, carefully checking my knees for scrapes and brushing the dust off my legs. With laughter in his blue eyes, he looked at me and asked, "Are you OK?"

Red-faced with embarrassment, I quickly replied, "Yeah, I'm fine," and rode away.

We lived in a small bungalow on Montcalm Avenue, only eight short blocks from the soccer field. Although I was only nine years old, I had spent the summer riding my bike all over our town, and Dad was confident I wouldn't get lost—well, as long as I looked where I was going. It was 1976, and parents back then weren't concerned with abductions or where we kids were most of the time. In fact, my mother's favorite saying was, "Go out and play. I don't want to see you kids until dinner!"

My parents were quite proud of our home in Saint Bruno, having lived only in apartments until that fateful day three years prior when they made their adult leap into a mortgage.

It was a modest redbrick home with a gray-shingled roof and an attached carport. Two small concrete steps led to a rather plain white door centered on the front of the house. The living room featured a wood-burning brick fireplace and a large, curved window that was divided into vertical panes through which you could see the front lawn. A narrow hallway to the left of the front door led to three bedrooms featuring the same vertical-paned windows and one small bathroom. By far, the fireplace was the most treasured feature of our home. Watching wood burn is therapeutic for the human soul and seems to calm even the most frantic mind. I valued its effect on my young parents, although at times, I would worry when a calm stare turned into a glazed trance. Given how many times our parents forgot to open the flue—causing smoke to billow ominously around our living room—it is a wonder we never burned down the house.

Our fireplace earned a place of honor on the many winter nights when the electricity failed. In Quebec, most homes are heated with baseboard electric, and most hydro lines are above ground—a combination that begs for power outages. Quebecers used to joke that when birds flapped their wings too quickly in Montreal, Hydro Quebec would lose power. I personally loved those winter nights when white, fluffy snow swirled around the house and neighbors would arrive, blankets in hand, to curl up in front of our fireplace. We kids would sleep close to the fire while the parents talked quietly by candlelight, waiting for a storm to subside or for some transformer to be repaired. Truth be told, I suspected some of the neighbors maintained cordial relations with us throughout the year because they knew the tremendous value of our fireplace when our street was without power at minus fifteen degrees Fahrenheit.

It was about 5:30 p.m. when I finally arrived home from Earl's game, having made a few stops to pet neighborhood dogs and buy candy at the local *dépanneur*. To my surprise, Madame Beaudoin, a neighbor who lived on the circle at the end of our street, was sitting on our front doorstep. She had been waiting for me. I was to come with her "*immédiatement*" and sleep over at her house, as my mother was "*occupée*."

I knew the Beaudoins well. My parents had spent many an evening at their house, smoking and talking politics over bottles of wine. In Quebec, spirited debates over political issues are relished rather than avoided, and wine was always a part of the conversation—a cultural necessity, if you will. Pulling out a bottle was considered a warm welcome to those who sat at your kitchen table, inviting them to stay awhile, to smoke, and to chat.

The Beaudoins were good Catholics with seven children, so my brother and I usually had someone to play with on any given evening. Madame Beaudoin was a short, portly woman with huge, watermelon-sized breasts—the type of breasts young girls don't wish for and young boys fear being smothered by. Like many Quebec women, she followed French fashion and was determined to look stylish at all times. Her hair was dyed a deep-auburn color and kept cropped short above the ears. Dark-rimmed, narrow glasses framed her friendly blue eyes, while heavy costume jewelry, meticulously selected to match whatever she was wearing, adorned her thick fingers and wrists. Around her neck she always wore a silver necklace with matching silver cross, though I noticed on certain occasions, the necklace was hidden under a silk scarf.

Madame seemed to have a large collection of scarves in every color, pattern, and motif, ready to add flair to her solid-color pantsuits. Quebec women have a sense of style and take pride in their appearance even when performing unglamorous tasks like grocery shopping or tanking up the car. Mr. Beaudoin, on the other hand, did not look like he belonged at all with Madame, as he was a thin, wiry man with a weathered face that spoke of hard labor, much smoking, and plenty of time spent outdoors. He always wore jeans and red lumberjack shirts—except on Sundays, when Madame insisted he put on his black slacks and a white shirt for Mass. At church, Madame would sit excitedly in her pew, intently listening to the priest and smiling graciously at her neighbors, while Mr. Beaudoin, his hands folded meekly in his lap, would stare blankly at the back of the pew in front of him. As the sermon wore on, he often would tap his feet as if counting the minutes down to the moment of his release. You see, he wasn't really interested in how Jesus fed two fish to the multitudes—he simply wanted to go fishing.

That night, after Madame herded me quickly over to their house, the Beaudoins seemed oddly quiet, and rather than them pulling out a board game or deck of cards after dinner, I was told to watch TV until bedtime. One of their older sons gave up his room for my use. I didn't suspect anything was seriously wrong until shortly after I went to bed. Without a knock, Madame Beaudoin burst into the bedroom. Her eyes were teary, and she immediately knelt beside the bed, set her hands in the prayer position, and motioned me to do the same. Getting out from under the bed covers, I obediently knelt beside her, my hands in prayer position against the bed, my eyes closed. There followed a long, long silence. Finally, after she choked back tears, I heard her say in the most solemn voice, "Let us pray...let us pray for your father."

At first, I thought Madame was expressing her deep love of God, but then I realized she meant *my* father and not the "our father" in heaven. My little body froze, and I couldn't get up the courage to speak. Madame Beaudoin's voice was equally paralyzed, and she left without a word. My father had died, I was somehow sure of it. I spent the night going over the details of that afternoon in my mind. "Are you OK?" were the last words my father ever said to me.

In the morning, all the Beaudoins had assumed monastic silence, and after finishing my cereal, I was hastily sent home. Although the walk from their house to ours was only about five hundred yards, it was the longest, loneliest walk I've ever made. I kept thinking, *Maybe I was wrong. Maybe Dad is* *still alive. Maybe he was paralyzed in some car accident on the way home from the game. No, he must have died...*As I rounded the corner, I could see my mother standing at our front door, waiting for me. Madame Beaudoin had obviously called her to tell her I was on my way. My mother's eyes were full of pain and dread. She quickly ushered me into the master bedroom, closed the door, and with a rain of tears, explained how the events of the day before had unfolded.

Shortly after I had left my father at the soccer field, there was a half-time break. While the teams rested and strategized, Dad had decided to jog around the track that circled the field. Over the years, his sweet tooth had thickened his waistline, and he was determined to return to swimsuit-ready shape. On a health kick, Dad had recently quit smoking and started exercising regularly. Lacking the stamina of a regular runner, he would often stop to rest and then drop down onto the track to sweat through a few push-ups or sit-ups. It was shortly after the second half began that Earl suddenly noticed that Dad didn't get up after a set of sit-ups. He ran over to my father, who was lying very still and flat on his back. Realizing it was serious, Earl screamed for help. Other parents rushed over, and an ambulance was called. There was no hope, though. Our father had died of a massive heart attack. He was thirty-seven years old.

"Dagny, I'm so sorry, so sorry!" Mom wailed, holding me tight in her arms. She then sat me down on the bed and held my hands in hers as she explained, "Your father died last night of a heart attack. The cause was atherosclerosis, which means his heart stopped working because blood got clogged in his artery." I wasn't quite sure what an artery was and wondered how often this type of thing happened to people, but it didn't matter. My deepest fear now confirmed, I burst into tears, and Mother, seeing my devastation, became angrier and angrier. "The stupid health care system in this province!" she yelled. "That ambulance took fifteen minutes to get to him! If they had come earlier, he might have been saved. I never told you this, Dagny, but a few weeks back, your father was feeling chest pains and sweating too much when he exercised. He was feeling real bad one day last week, and I convinced him to go to the emergency room. You know what the hospital staff said? You know what those jerks said to him? They asked him if he had ever had a heart attack. When he said no, they explained that the nurses were on strike and that he should come back to the hospital after the strike was over for tests. That was three days ago! Maybe if they had run those tests, they could have saved him!"

"And, to make matters worse, he had quit smoking, the fool! Everyone says smoking is bad for you, but I think the smoking was keeping his blood thin. If he hadn't quit, maybe his blood wouldn't have thickened and clogged his arteries!" After wiping her tears with her sleeves, she finally blurted out, "Oh God, Dagny, I'm so sorry! You know the real reason I think he died? The real reason? The night before he died, I fed him hot dogs! Can you believe that? What a terrible wife I am. It was the hot dogs that killed him!" Just as I was making a solemn vow never to eat hot dogs again, Mom started to yell erratically at the family dog, who had taken refuge under the bed. "Get out from there, you stupid dog, get out!" Mom seemed upset that our mangy poodle-terrier dog, the dog that spent countless hours digging holes in our backyard, could somehow exist in this world while her husband had died.

Like everyone else, in the days that followed his passing, I focused on all the things I loved about my father. We humans improve with death, as our family and friends are gracious enough to focus only on the positive. At the age of nine, children can be selfish. I wasn't concerned with how the loss would affect my mother or my brother or anyone else, for that matter. I was only concerned with how the loss of my father would affect me. And it seemed clear to me that God had made a big mistake. He had taken the wrong parent. You see, my father had had a playfulness about him that charmed everyone, and while Mother took the business of living quite seriously, my dad seemed to value fun over everything else. Of course, children only interpret a parent's priorities by what they see them do day in and day out. Mom's work seemed to include paying the bills, housecleaning, cooking, grocery shopping, laundry, worrying, and disciplining us kids. Dad's chores seemed to be limited to studying, lawn maintenance, and snow shoveling, all of which left him a good deal more time to spend with us.

Unlike many fathers, Dad truly loved spending time with us kids. I remember at the beginning of every Quebec winter, he would build Earl an ice rink with plywood sides in the backyard and help him practice hockey. When the snow was deep enough, he spent countless hours pulling our heavy wooden toboggan up hills so that Earl and I, with Dad as anchor and brakeman, could fly downhill, screaming with laughter. In the summer, Dad built us tree forts and often shuttled all the neighborhood kids and their bikes to the top of the steepest hill in town so we could race down it. He taught us kids how to paddle a canoe and led us on long hikes through the Laurentian Mountains. On a whim, and much to my mother's dismay, he would often bring home puppies, kittens, and, on one occasion, even cute yellow ducks. He worked part-time at a car dealership, and arriving home on winter nights, he would often sneak into my bedroom, kiss me good-night, and place his cold hands on my cheeks to make me giggle. And sometimes, in the dead of winter and against Mom's wishes, he would let Earl or me sit on his lap and steer our Volkswagen beetle down the back streets of our town.

The most unforgettable thing Dad ever did was steal me from school. My father was studying religion and philosophy at Loyola College and planned to be a teacher. Occasionally, his own classes would be canceled, and he'd find himself with a free afternoon. On these days, he would sometimes go to the administrative office of my elementary school and explain that there had been a tragedy in the family or some sickness had befallen someone and that I was to be immediately taken home. With grave seriousness, I was pulled out of class by a teacher, and Dad would keep up the farce until he got me into the car. He would then burst out laughing, explain the story, and take me to a local playground and push me on the swings for hours or balance me high on the teeter-totter. Most often, we would end up at McDonald's, talking and sharing a milk shake.

The idea that my father, when he had spare time, wanted to spend it with me was the best gift he ever gave me. Mother would eventually hear about my absence from school and berate my father. Dad would sit there listening to her sermonize about the importance of my education and how irresponsible he was as a parent. "You're teaching that child to tell fibs too!" Dad, his eyes glued to the floor, seemed to solemnly accept his punishment. However, as soon as Mom marched out of the room, he would look over at me with a mischievous grin and give me a wink that said, *We had fun, didn't we!*

The only day of the week when Dad seemed adult-like was Sunday. He would get up early, put on a suit and tie, and take Earl and me to the Catholic church to hear Mass. Mom never joined us, as she always said Sundays were her only day off, her only time to rest.

Now, at the funeral home, I stared at Dad's lifeless body and held the obituary they distributed as you entered the room tight in my little hands. His name—Klaus Paul Sladeczek—was emblazoned in gold letters across the top of the paper. Dad seemed much too handsome and young to be lying in white satin. I had never been to a funeral or seen an open casket, but having spent countless hours at church, I knew resurrections were possible. It also seemed to me that given the event was called a "wake," there was some possibility Dad would wake up. I spent the entire time praying fervently he would simply sit up, hoping that this was all some practical joke on his part.

Until the day of the funeral, I had no idea how well loved my father was in the community, as the quite sizable church was standing room only. My mother spent most of the funeral consoling her own mother. Everyone used to say that Nana thought the sun rose and set on my father, and her grief seemed unrelenting. Dad's best friend, Fritz, stood with head bowed by the casket, holding his hands together in a tight grip, not wanting to leave Dad's side. Fritz and my father had arrived in Montreal via the Europa-Canada Line on the MS *Seven Seas* back in 1958. I had seen a black-and-white photo of my father and Fritz on the bow of that ship, dressed in suits with narrow ties, looking tired from the long journey but eager to begin their new lives in Canada. They were best buddies. I'll never forget the countless hours Fritz and my father spent hunched over a game of chess—both deep in concentration, both determined to checkmate. Later in the church as the priest delivered the eulogy, Fritz seemed to sink deeper into an abyss. He was fully shattered, not having come to grips with the loss.

At the time of my father's death, my mother was vice-principal of a large high school in Saint Hubert, Quebec—not an insignificant feat for a woman in the 1970s. For four years, Dad had been studying and working toward getting a teacher's certificate. The thinking was that once Dad became a teacher and secured a steady job, Mom could trade places with him and spend more time with us kids. A month prior to his death, Dad finally finished his studies. Since then, he had been applying for full-time teaching positions at English-language Catholic school boards in and around Montreal. It was at 2:00 p.m. on July 8, only a few hours before his death, that he accepted an offer for a full-time position as a teacher of religious studies. Yes, life can sometimes kick you in the teeth. For me, the fun parent was gone forever, and my future seemed a dark, black, unwritten page.

After the funeral, friends and family poured into our small house. Many women in the neighborhood had made time to cook, and food appeared seemingly out of nowhere. After a somber dinner at which no one spoke above a whisper, I was sent to bed. I didn't understand the laughter that slowly began filtering through the walls. Like at an Irish wake, as the evening wore on, people started to tell funny stories about my father to celebrate his life. Not being able to make out the stories, all I could hear was laughter, so for much of the night, I lay in bed thinking, *Am I the only one in this family that is truly sad my father died?* I eventually cried myself to sleep, holding on to the only thing left in my young life that seemed worth living for—a picture of a horse.

3

A Sea Change

My mother planned her exit carefully. There is no doubt that the idea of leaving Quebec had dripped through her mind before, but Dad would never have allowed it. My mother always had itchy feet, but my father, like most Germans, preferred to be securely rooted to a place. That didn't matter now, though. As a widow, Mom was at the helm, and we kids were crewmembers at best, just along for the sail and not really knowing where the wind would blow us. It was late one evening after dinner when Mom casually announced that we were moving, lock, stock, and barrel, to Ontario. Both dazed, Earl and I just stared wide-eyed as she explained her reasons.

First, she said angrily, "You know I can't take the politics of this province anymore!" Earl and I knew what she was referring to. For many months now, every adult conversation had been focused on the provincial election. You see, political power in Quebec had changed, and we Anglophones (English speakers) were on the short end of the stick. It seemed the French were no longer content to be worker bees, and they certainly didn't want to be second-class citizens in their own province. In November 1976, they finally turned the tables on us Anglophones, electing the Parti Québécois to power.

It was said that the French, being Catholic and partial to large families, had bred us English out of power, democracy being so strongly linked with sheer volume. During the campaign, the PQ had promised that if elected, they would have a referendum to decide Quebec's future. As my mother explained, "If the PQ wins the referendum, Quebec will no longer be part of Canada." Having recently memorized where Canada's ten provinces and two territories were on the map, it seemed to me the loss of Quebec would leave a rather big hole in Canada and be terribly inconvenient for the eastern provinces, those provinces way over on the right-hand side of the map.

To make matters worse, a few months after the election, Bill 101 began pushing Anglophones into French-language schools. Tired of it all, Mom wanted to stomp language issues like a cigarette butt out of her life forever. She also had another, more personal, reason to leave. "Dad," she said, "was just too loved in Saint Bruno." One wouldn't think that being too loved would ever amount to a problem in this life. But everywhere Mom turned, even at the grocery store, people would see her and start sobbing, remembering my father. Rather than take comfort in their sorrow and shared remembering, Mom apparently needed a blank page on which to write the next chapter of her life. For Earl and me, the sea change hit us like an ocean wave.

Only a few weeks later, a giant Allied Van Lines truck was parked in front of our house, ready to uproot us. It took the movers only half a day to load all of our possessions into barely one-third of the enormous vehicle. All that day, Mother put on a brave face, trying to be pleasant with the movers as they packed up her memories. When the truck did finally pull away, we were stripped to the essentials: a car, the three of us, and our mangy poodle-terrier dog. No one spoke as we took a last look at 1163 Montcalm Avenue. Mom paused for a moment as she sat behind the wheel, took a deep breath, and started the car. It was the end of the first scene of our lives. And, just like at a final curtain call, we knew the drapes wouldn't reopen.

Once you exit Montreal, the long drive up the 401 Highway towards St. Catharines, Ontario (our new hometown) has to be one of the most boring drives on the planet. The highway, often dead straight, is edged with wide swaths of grass and trees, trees, and more trees for hours on end. With Kelly the dog resting comfortably on my lap, I watched

Mom navigate the busy lanes and listened as she cursed the many eighteen-wheelers trying to bully our smallish Plymouth Volaré. For seven hours, her hands clenched the wheel and never varied from the official ten o'clock and two o'clock positions. It was not nervousness but determination and will. Although she relished the freedom to make all the decisions in her life, she also bore the weight of them on her shoulders. She had visibly aged since my father had died. Smoking more heavily now, she had whittled down to about 115 pounds, and her skin seemed dry and sallow. I noticed her short, reddish-brown hair had become fringed with steely gray. Now that she was husbandless, perhaps there was no real reason to dye it.

It seemed to me, even back then, that Mom's path through life had always been a rocky one. We had heard stories of her alcoholic father and her mother's strong preference for her older brothers. Lucky for us, whatever darts life threw at her seemed to make her stronger. She still hadn't found a job in our new town, but Earl and I weren't worried about that. Mom would look after us "come hell or high water," as she always said. For her, work was the solution to all life's problems. Even when she looked tired, a nervous energy seemed to propel her forward.

The drive, as life changing as it was, had locked the three of us into an eerie quiet. It was a good three hours before Mom tried to break the silence. Knowing Earl was upset at having to leave his friends and hockey team behind, she tried to put a positive spin on things when she suddenly piped up, "I think you two will both like St. Catharines. You have your great aunt Edna and Mabel there, and Earl, you're just about your cousin Joanne's age. You remember meeting Joanne once in Ottawa, don't you? And St. Catharines won't be as cold as Montreal, and you'll get to have so many new adventures, meet new people, make new friends."

"Right," Earl said with bitterness, looking out the car window. "I'm sure it will be just peachy." Earl was angry with the world. He had lost his father, and now all his friends were gone too. In a way, I was the lucky one. Being an introverted child, I was more likely to be found playing with neighborhood dogs or drawing pictures of horses than actually speaking with people. As such, I had no particular friends to miss.

"Mom," I ventured. "You said I could ride, right?"

"Yes, Dagny, I promise I will find a barn you can ride at," replied my mother. That was enough to put my heart at ease, as I knew she would keep her word. My mother was not the easiest person to live with, but she always kept her promises—it was the thing I liked best about her. For me, it really didn't matter anymore where the road led, for I had a cherished human condition to ground me—a goal. It was lucky for me that sometimes goals are portable, not tied to a particular place. A goal can help a person through a difficult time, as it gives the mind a point to focus on, and that focus allows the rest of life to blur a little.

Dad's death had reinforced in me the notion that life could be short and perhaps it was a good idea to achieve something. After all, I was ten now and no longer in the single digits. After considerable thought and reflection, I decided with utter seriousness that life would be a worthless series of days if I didn't become an exceptional horseback rider. Like Elizabeth Taylor in *National Velvet*, I would overcome all my troubles and win. All I had to do was practice and my riding skill would be there for all the world to see, and I would be happy in the seeing.

It seems my early dabbles in music, art, and soccer had led me to believe that having a hobby you are good at is important. I suppose if, as a child, I had been shuttled around to volunteer at soup kitchens, I would have learned that helping others is a priority. No, in truth, becoming a great rider wasn't, and isn't, a very important goal in the grand scheme of things—I mean, it's not quite like establishing world peace or finding the cure for cancer. In fact, in terms of practicality, horseback riding is much like downhill skiing. The goal of a downhill skier is to get from the top of a large, snow-packed mountain to the bottom at breakneck speed *without* breaking one's neck—or being buried by an equally fast avalanche. Unless you are talented enough to teach others to ski or can capitalize on an Olympic-medal win, downhill skiing is not a very pragmatic skill. I mean, when is being able to glide down a hill at eighty miles per hour practical?

But then again, hobbies, sports, and pastimes don't need to be practical—they must only amuse, feed our competitive spirit, and stroke our egos' need to distinguish ourselves from the billions of other people who populate this strange, blue planet. Think for a moment about the Olympic high jump. Initially, when the sport first came into being, the athlete would use a scissor kick to get over the pole. It was only when Dick Fosbury won the 1968 Gold Medal with his ingenious flop backward over the pole that high-jump athletes were inspired to leap backward to soar to greater heights. After careful reflection, I can't think of any practical application for jumping as high as you can over a pole and landing on the back of your neck and shoulders. No, the high jump represents pure human fun—just a way to say, "I can jump higher than you can!"

Riding horses is also a very strange thing for a human to be fixated on. You may never have thought about it, but horses are grazing animals not meant to be ridden. It was lucky for them that their bodies had a strong midsection we humans could wrap our legs around. I say *lucky* because if horses weren't as beautiful as they are or if we humans couldn't ride them, I'm sure we would have eaten more of them. I do admit that I sometimes daydream about the giraffe. They would have been so much fun to ride if they just didn't have such a sloping back and if we humans were tall enough to mount them without a scaffold! With their fashionable stripes, zebras would have also made stunning mounts. However, zebras are not stupid and are curiously skilled at avoiding the ropes humans use to try to catch them. Not only are zebras difficult to catch, they also have a nasty habit of biting deeply into the human arm and not letting go. Horses, on the other hand, had the proper anatomy, and they could, with some training or bullying, be duped into letting us ride them.

I sometimes wonder about that first brave soul who decided to hop on a horse. Maybe he did it on a dare. I'm sure it was a he, probably about sixteen years old. Or perhaps that first rider was merely entrepreneurial, having observed that a horse could get from point A to point B much faster than a human could walk and thinking that that might be to some advantage. While horses were beasts of burden for much of human history (plowing fields and providing much-needed public transportation), they are now decommissioned, outdated, and (apart from police work, ranch work, and tourist hauls) retired from active duty. In sum, horses are now, generally, pets. Learning to ride an eleven-hundred-pound animal with a mind of its own, an animal that can gallop twenty-five to thirty miles per hour, and an animal that will, on occasion, try to strategically propel you from its back, is now simply a brilliant human leisure activity.

At the age of ten, with my first real goal now carefully hung on the inner wall of my mind, I felt as straight as a ship in a channel. I was proud to have a goal—it felt so purposeful, so adultlike. Little did I know that we humans are ambitious, goal-setting machines. Some people want to tempt fate and climb Mount Everest. For others, that is mere child's play—for them, only climbing Mount Everest without oxygen merits praise. For me, oxygen seems like such a necessity, like that small bottle of mouthwash that shouldn't be forgotten on a business trip. Golfers focus on hitting small, white balls into tiny holes strategically placed far, far away yet always conveniently marked with a thin flagpole. Many people dedicate their lives to achieving corporate success. Some climb the corporate ladder even when they suspect it is leaning against the wrong wall. Mothers put their own needs selflessly aside and pursue practical goals like succeeding at potty training a child. Of course, there are the inspired types who support worthy causes like protecting the environment, saving animals from abuse, or helping the poor. Politicians are gutsy and willing to take on the bigger problems, like reducing the unemployment rate or the national debt. And there are those who feel that they are just not up to those grander goals. Perhaps it stems from a lack of confidence, or maybe they've self-assessed, taken stock of their personal assets and liabilities, and decided, realistically, hey, perhaps they should be more reasonable with their goal setting. These cautious types take on relatively achievable goals, like repainting their living rooms or mastering their digital movie cameras. And finally, there are those who pursue goals that are quite beyond their capabilities and for which they have no real talent. They then pursue these goals with obsessive diligence, hoping upon hope that pure determination will get them there. I, sadly, fall into this latter category.

Within a few weeks of arriving in Ontario, Mom explained that things were "tight" and that I would have to pitch in to pay for my riding lessons. She found a barn I could ride at where the owners were willing to barter stall mucking and horse feeding for lessons. Only in the horse world where a young girl's love of horses is so, so, strong can barn owners extract such a deal. Mucking stalls is such heavy work—equivalent to asking a boy to shovel a parking lot full of snow for his hockey practice. Heck, at hockey games, the boys just sit around and watch the Zamboni machine clean the ice.

The deal Mom signed me up for also suspiciously involved dropping me off at the barn early on Saturday mornings and picking me up in the evening. (Hmmm...what did Mom do all those Saturdays?) Nevertheless, I wanted so much to ride, I probably would have thrown housework into the bargain if anyone had asked. Since I was already well trained for horse slave labor, the barn owners were delighted to have me. Indeed, I was a neurotic young teenager who could be counted on to triple-check that all the water buckets were full, that every horse was fed, the stalls cleaned, fence doors securely latched, and all tools were returned to their rightful places. Although I was physically small, I had the determination of a bulldog. It didn't matter if a bale of hay weighed twice what I did; with careful balancing, a deep breath, and a good deal of propulsion, a full bale of hay could be moved with a wheelbarrow. Heavy buckets of water could also be delivered slowly and patiently if I just stopped every ten feet for a brief rest.

Despite the heavy labor that made me look like a stocky body builder, I was happy. I loved spoiling the horses with carrots, rubbing their foreheads, brushing their long manes and tails, and lending them my hands when they needed that itchy part under their manes scratched. At feeding time, I looked forward to listening to them shove their noses excitedly into their grain buckets. Even watching horses eat hay is delightful, as their rhythmic chewing seems to lead them into a meditative trance. Yes, barn life was perfect as far as I was concerned, and I already had my second life goal—I wanted a barn of my own one day and was saving my allowance. I already had twelve dollars, so things were looking up. Of course, the road of life doesn't always take you where you expect to go.

As I grew older, we moved from city to city for no apparent reason. It seemed my mother's itchy feet had turned into some sort of athlete's-foot condition. My brother and I would first sense a move was coming when Mom would start rearranging the furniture. This stage was always followed by the renovation stage. Unlike the kids of other mothers, it would be more usual for my brother and me to find ours knocking down a kitchen's wall rather than actually cooking in it. This woman could drywall, tape, plaster, paint, tile, recalk bathrooms, and even make furniture, but she couldn't seem to prepare anything more complicated than Kraft Dinner or grilled cheese. Of course, once the renovation phase was over, once she got our house just the way she wanted, we would move—because, apparently, that is very logical. To her credit, in every new town we settled, Mom would find me a new riding school.

Over the years, I enjoyed many lessons and attended weekend horse clinics. Despite all this training, however, my riding skill remained—how should I say—uninspiring. In fact, I was particularly good at placing fifth in any horse-show competition I entered. Given there were typically only four or five riders per class, fifth usually meant dead last. My mother attended every show with the enthusiasm that only a mother can muster and congratulated me with big hugs for every fifth-place ribbon I received. "Congratulations! I'm so proud of you. Wow, fifth! Fifth place! Very well done!"

I did receive a first-place ribbon once, and only once. It was a jumping class. Had I improved at last, you ask? No. I won the jumping class because the course was muddy that day, and every other rider fell off. Yes, I was the only child who finished the course in one piece and still on board the mount. After receiving my first-place ribbon, I proudly glanced into the stands and caught my mother and riding instructor looking at each other in utter disbelief. Disappointed, I quickly wiped their shock from my mind, for I was sure this shiny, *finally blue*, ribbon was a sign that I was a better rider. You can imagine the swallowed tears when at the next horse show, I placed fifth.

About once a year, my mother would insist Earl "support" his little sister by attending one of my shows. I really don't know how she bribed attendance out of him. At one show, he arrived late, and I spotted him at the edge of the riding ring. Having just finished an equitation class, I rode up to him on my borrowed school horse, fifth-place ribbon in hand, to say hello. Now a cheeky teenager, Earl looked at me with a mocking grin and said, "So, you like riding in circles, eh? Very exciting. What do you do for an encore? Ride counterclockwise?"

I was furious. "No," I protested. "Riding is harder than it looks!" And I trotted off, wishing he had stayed home. Deep down, I must admit his smart-alecky comment made me giggle. Riding does involve going in circles. As students, we orbit around our instructors for years. Even when we test our skills at horse shows, we go in circles—I suppose this is designed to prepare us to go straight one day.

I have a great deal of respect for the wisdom of the standard—firmly enclosed with gate shut—riding ring. In fact, I suspect most mothers and fathers who innocently bring their children for their first riding lessons have no idea how dangerous riding is. Why do we ride in enclosed and well-fenced rings with no obvious exits? Because leaving the gate open is tantamount to inviting the horse to leave, usually with a quick, premeditated dash on its part—with or without your child—to return to its horse buddies or the freedom of the pasture. You see, horses don't really enjoy going in circles. Of course, if they're confined to a small stall all day with little freedom, being in a large riding ring and going in circles might seem infinitely better. If horses had their way, I suspect they would prefer to live very unconfined lives together in large, tasty, green pastures. Yes, I sometimes think horses would be utterly content if their interaction with humans was limited to us bringing them grain, filling their water troughs, and occasionally brushing the caked mud off of their itchy fur.

Throughout my teens, I bartered horse slave labor for lessons at a barn about twenty minutes' drive from our home. One Saturday afternoon, John, the stable owner, asked me to add clean shavings to three empty stalls. "We have some new boarders arriving today," he explained.

"Sure, no problem," I replied and quickly set about hauling the large, seemingly vacuum-packed shavings into the stalls. I always enjoyed spreading fresh shavings. To spread it evenly, you have to kick it around like a pile of fall leaves, which is a lot of fun, and when you're done, the stall smells like a clean hamster cage. A bed of shavings is a fluffy, white mattress to a horse. Although horses do not sleep as much as humans do—averaging only about three hours of sleep in twenty-four—and they mostly sleep standing up, they will sometimes lie down to rest. It is the funniest thing to watch a horse lying on its side, sound asleep in a stall and snoring gently, its feet twitching from a dream! When horses do lie down, they are such big animals that a lot of pressure is put on their hocks and elbows. Shavings are soft and help keep the horse from chafing those sensitive, thin-skinned parts. Shavings also act much like kitty litter, if you know what I mean.

LIFE WITHOUT STIRRUPS

As I worked, I thought, *What a funny word "boarders" is.* I had recently looked it up in the dictionary to find it means "one who pays a stipulated sum in return for regular meal or meals and lodging." Certainly, anyone who owns a horse knows that regular, stipulated sums are required at every turn. Of course, there is the monthly board fee, which can range from $200 to $600 a month depending on how fancy the facility is. However, the cost of board is just the beginning and certainly doesn't include "horsey" incidentals. For example, every eight weeks, a horse needs a pedicure, which involves having a farrier come out to the barn to trim its feet. Yes, those hard-shelled hooves grow like human toenails and need to be trimmed back regularly. Many horses have horseshoes hammered into their soles at the same time. This doesn't hurt the horse, but it does hurt the pocketbook, being equivalent to buying a child a new pair of Adidases every other month.

Horses also need to be wormed, or "dewormed," if you will. Apparently, eating all that grass and hay has some drawbacks, and one has to keep the horse's intestines clean of nasty critters! Giving a horse a wormer involves shoving a short tube into its mouth and trying to squirt the wormer paste in before the horse backs up, raises its head too high, or spits it out on the ground. Horses can be pretty tricky and will stand quietly, pretending they've swallowed the gunk, only to spit it out as soon as you walk away! Sneaking up on the horse, hiding the tube behind your back, and trying to get the wormer in its mouth before it knows what you are doing, is, believe it or not, the recommended method.

Then there is the cost of biannual vaccinations and other vet visits to address injuries. Horses seem to like to hurt themselves. If you let a horse out on a ten-acre pasture and there is a rusted tractor tucked away in one corner of the field, no doubt the horse will find a way to injure itself on it. And then there are the bottles of fly spray that need to be purchased, along with many creams and liniments...

Just as I was thinking about the cost of horse ownership, the new boarders pulled up in front of the barn. *Well, that horse trailer certainly cost a pretty penny!* I thought. In front of the barn was what can only be described as a kick-ass horse trailer. It was polished to perfection and pulled by a heavy-duty and equally spiffy diesel truck. Three pretty blond girls, each with their hair tied back with black ribbons, jumped from the backseat of the truck while their parents secured the trailer wheels with chocks. Clearly, they had just come from a horse show, as they were still wearing their white shirts; cream-colored breeches; and tall, shiny, black leather dressage boots. The girls unloaded their horses with the confidence that shouts experience. I had never ever seen such magnificent animals. These horses looked in the peak of condition; their coats shone, not a hair was out of place, and each of their obviously valuable legs was carefully protected with white leg wraps.

I was standing at the barn entrance as they walked by and offered my warmest "Welcome to Reber Ridge!" The girls, though it was obvious they had heard me, chose to say nothing and sauntered past as if I didn't exist. Even the horses seemed to flaunt their shiny hooves as they walked by me.

John told the girls, "Dagny helps us on Saturdays, and she has your stalls all ready for you." The girls glanced over at me and seemed to size me up from head to toe. I suddenly felt very self-conscious. Embarrassed, I looked down and stared at my farmer-style rubber boots. They certainly weren't like their shiny leather ones! It was then that I noticed my red plaid shirt was covered with pieces of hay, shavings, and what appeared to be horse snot. Nervously, I began picking out the hay and was angry at myself for letting the barn's black Lab jump all over me, as my pants were covered with a fine layer of black hair.

Just as I was almost finished wiping the worst of the hay and hair off of my clothing, one of the girls walked past me and said laughingly, "Don't forget to give our horses grain, tomboy!" All three then started to giggle as they walked away.

Stunned and insulted, I stood there pathetically without saying a word. It was just then that Mary, a very nice girl that I shared group lessons with, walked up and said, "I heard all three of those Spencer girls have been taking privates for years, and they are really excellent riders. They clean up at all the shows."

Great, I thought, *they have their* very own *horses,* and *they get private lessons,* and *they are excellent riders*! Up to that point, my efforts to convince my mother to buy me a horse had failed miserably. Oh, I had asked mother to buy me a horse for Christmas. She, in her awe-inspiring wisdom, bought me a telescope. As I unpacked the contraption, I couldn't help thinking that a scientific instrument is very unlike a horse! In all my years of riding, I had never had a private lesson with an instructor. Apparently, one full day of Saturday slave labor equaled one group horseback riding lesson. It was at that very moment that it finally dawned on me. *Oh my God, I'm poor—or, at best, lower middle class!* Up until then, I was completely clueless about my social status, but now the realization hit me like a winter freeze. We couldn't afford a horse, and I couldn't afford privates, and private lessons were obviously the missing piece I needed to win blue ribbons!

Doubt began to drip like a faucet and filled my mind. I spent the rest of that summer testing a theory. I wanted to see if, despite a lack of resources, I could excel at riding. Unfortunately, by the time the first reds of autumn arrived, I had no first-place ribbons to proudly pin on a bedroom wall.

One Saturday, just as my group lesson was winding down, I lost my stirrups while cantering and ended up face first in the arena dust. As luck would have it, at that very moment, the eldest of the pretty Spencer girls entered the ring for her private lesson. As I was slowly lifting myself out of the dirt with my hands and elbows, she let her horse walk right past my head, and I heard her say with a smirk, "Find anything interesting down there, tomboy?" I was brokenhearted and ashamed. If horseback riding was something I was not good at and if riding was too expensive a hobby anyway, what was the point? *Why should I continue disappointing myself?* I thought. *I'll never be good at this!* I so wanted to be one of those girls getting first-place ribbons and winning those beautiful saddles, but I wasn't. I just had to accept that. Utterly discouraged, I did the unthinkable: I quit!

I was sixteen when I stopped riding. It was almost like I had stopped breathing. Great expectations: what a curse they are. I didn't talk about my decision to anyone. I'm sure my mother thought I had simply lost interest in horses. I don't think she ever understood the depth of my self-created disappointment. For many years, I couldn't look at a horse without feeling a dreadful pang in my heart. If I caught a glimpse of a horse alongside a road, I would look away. If I saw a horse on TV, I would change the channel. I didn't want to see even a small reminder of the riding life I had once loved.

4

Lurching Forward

*F*ourteen years later...

What I'd *really* like to say is that I graduated from university *magna cum laude*, that my stunning law career snapped me from my working-class roots, and that the law firm I worked for was so impressed with my intellect that I was made full partner by the time I was thirty years old. However, that would be a little fib.

Well, it's not entirely untrue. I did write the law-school entrance exam. Unfortunately, according to my painful LSAT results, I am not adept at solving abstract problems,

LIFE WITHOUT STIRRUPS

and neither, apparently, any problems that involve math or financial equations. Yes, I admit I have difficulty answering questions like: *If a car's gas tank holds fifteen gallons and consumes gas at a rate of one gallon every twenty miles and the tank is now one-quarter full, how far can you go before you have to tank up?* But I do understand these concepts on a more elementary level. When the needle on our car's fuel gauge gets close to the letter *E*, I tank up—if only to avoid the embarrassment of having to foot it to the nearest gas station. And, I'm proud to say, it only took a few patiently repeated explanations before I mastered the TV remote. So, as you can see, I'm not completely dense.

In fact, my suburban, middle-class, life has been peppered with a few accomplishments. I successfully housebroke a pair of miniature-schnauzer puppies—well, at least to the point where any accidents on their part were followed by appropriate doggy guilt and paw-pointing at each other. I fine-tuned my ability to remain perfectly calm while going through airport security. I've been cavity-free for years and even managed to memorize all sixteen digits of my Visa card, the expiration date, and that three-digit security code on the back. My greatest coup, however, was that I married someone smarter than me with good earning potential. And those LSAT test scorers thought I couldn't solve abstract financial problems!

Yes, I was very lucky. My husband and I had had the good fortune of meeting in high school. Looking back, I can now appreciate the advantages of meeting one's spouse young. For example, our combined wealth included two bicycles, so there was no need for a prenup. We had been relatively unfazed by life's hurts, so we jumped into our relationship with the optimism of new puppies. There is something pure and unfettered about two people who haven't lived enough to develop a hard shell or become set in their ways. Kam and I met in an English class—I was two rows over from his. He was a tall, gangly teenager and a math geek who always wore plaid shirts that he covered with a blue spandex jacket, while I was (and unfortunately, still am) a short, plain Jane with no particularly notable qualities. Even though his brown eyes were well hidden behind thick, dark-rimmed glasses, I could always see the smile in them. It only took a few cute glances and quiet grins to create an understanding between us. The year we graduated, Kam won nearly every academic award the school offered. I suspected even then, like our wedding song, that he would always be "the wind beneath my wings."

Unfortunately, by the time I graduated from university, my stars were not quite aligning. I had majored in political science. Apparently, while this education honed my thinking and writing skills, it left me sorely unprepared for the job market. There is something cruel about being able to think analytically about one's unemployment. After sending out hundreds of resumes, I landed an incredibly dull government job in downtown Toronto. How I ended up working in the tax policy department of the Ontario Ministry of Finance is still a mystery. Kam was particularly amused, for after I received the job offer, he looked at me with a smile and said, "Let's just hope they never ask you to calculate percentages."

Living as we were in suburbia, my life now included a three-hour-a-day stifling commute. First, there was the drive to the always packed GO train station, then the GO train journey to downtown (passing some very questionable neighborhoods, I might add), then a transfer to Toronto's subway system and a few subterranean stops, after which I finally rejoined the planet above ground for the ten-minute walk to the building I dreaded. Life had become a mundane series of never-ending circular steps: commute, work, return commute, a feeble attempt at dinner, bills, endless housecleaning, *repeat*.

Perhaps it was the fact that I was half German, but keeping household items in perfect order had become my new religion. Somehow, if the house was dust-free and the bathrooms were clean, sanity was assured. Sadly, long commutes and long hours at work can numb a human and squeeze life tightly, leaving little breathing room for the things that make the breathing worthwhile. It takes a bit of time, but an avid surfer can forget the rush of the ocean, former little ballerinas can forget the dance, and commuters can forget the power of galloping hooves. Yes, horses were now just a piece of my childhood puzzle—like a fond memory of a vacation long past (the rainy days that had blocked out the Caribbean sun had been long forgotten), and memories of my utter lack of riding talent, with time, had been softened and replaced in my mind with a remembrance of equestrian skill. Isn't it interesting how memories can evolve on their own accord, even sometimes converting fact to fiction?

Curiously, I decided to totally sidestep the child-rearing years. In a former life, I must have had too many children. No doubt I had once drowned myself in a fog-covered lake in despair of them, and the karma stayed with me in this life—for, even at the tender age of five, I shunned Barbie dolls and babies and declared sternly to my parents that I would *never* have children! My one and only babysitting experience as a teenager only deepened my resolve. The two-year-old I was watching ran like a mad person around every room, screaming and laughing at the same time. He taunted me by trying to put his fingers in light sockets, threw Legos in all directions, spilled food everywhere except into his mouth, and then gleefully crawled all over me with his Cheerio-stained shirt and smelly bottom. When I finally managed the acrobatic task of changing the boy's diaper while holding him tight to the changing table to prevent him from falling off, I thought the crib stage would be the easy part. After I listened to him scream for a full half hour, the little "angel" finally fell to sleep. For the rest of the evening, I walked up the stairs to the child's room at precisely ten-minute intervals to check that he was still breathing. There would be no baby deaths on my watch. Hours later, when the child's parents arrived looking refreshed and relaxed, they found me biting my nails and pacing the living room like a caged lion.

No, in truth, I never understood the joys of having children—the whole business seems much overrated. Furthermore, all the mirrors I've ever looked at confirm that my genes are neither of outstanding quality nor needed for the planet's success. Although I was blessed with my father's blue eyes, my hair is a mousy brown; I'm as flat chested as Sandra Bullock, my figure is shaped more like a pear than an hourglass, and I think if I was ever hooked to a cart, my wrestler-like legs could probably plough a field. No, my unwillingness to procreate would not be a loss to the gene pool. Like ants, we humans seem far too intent on population growth and mound building anyway. To me, looking after a dog or cat seemed a much easier and equally respectable alternative and would satisfy any smoldering maternal instinct—wherever it might be.

Of course, I had to grow accustomed to facing down the blank stares that followed the ever-present "Do you have any children?" question. The notion that a young married woman didn't have children aroused either sympathy ("They must be sterile") or consternation ("They must be selfish"). The idea that I didn't want any little cherubs running around the house was a great mystery to most. At first, to put people at ease, I'd respond with the vague "maybe someday." As the years passed, however, my husband and I came to appreciate the brilliance of our decision and now respond, "No, we don't have children. We're allergic to them." People just don't know what to make of this answer, and we quite enjoy watching them wonder whether we are pulling the wool over their eyes or if such an allergy is indeed possible.

Of course, when one has children, one's personal goals in life are patently clear: *Must bring up good children, not psychopaths,* who will eventually be able to leave the nest and fly solo without the warm comfort of our credit card. Childless, one's path through life is a little less charted. Perhaps it was guilt, but I dearly wanted to have an interesting answer to the all-important dinner-party question: "So, what do you do for fun?" I mean, something had to explain how I occupied all those child-free hours. I couldn't really answer that I clean my house with a task-based method—dusting and Windexing first, then vacuuming and mopping of floors, dreaded toilets always last—but then, on special occasions, I change things up and proceed room by room. No, the more riveting the answer to the dinner-party question, the more fascinating the person. Skydiving is always a hit at parties and implies you probably have more courage than anyone else standing in the room; playing a musical instrument is just plain sexy. Team sports can go either way—putting you in the "jock" or "athlete" category depending on the sport. Quilting implies creativity with slightly neurotic tendencies. I once heard a man sheepishly admit at a dinner party that reading was his hobby. "I know it sounds boring," he said, "but I read in my spare time." Goodness gracious, what a thought! Reading!

I took up painting for a while. Of course, I immediately envisioned the future art shows where my work would be prominently displayed and receive much whispered praise. Always one to jump right in, I enrolled in art classes and spent countless hours in art stores buying every shade of paint imaginable, the best brushes, only the finest-quality paper and, of course, the classic easel! Madame Rousseau, my childhood art teacher, would have been impressed with the now more varied palette. After spending a week's pay on supplies and a few classes, I was surprised to learn that "art" does indeed require some talent, patience, and practice—yes, real practice. Seriously? Have you ever looked at a Jackson Pollock? Before too long, it was my sincerest hope that in the middle of the night, my art supplies would come to life and paint masterpieces all by their lonesome.

Given the long commute and the fact that I was glued to an office desk much of the workday, I thought a more physical hobby might do the trick. One year, I was particularly inspired by Olympic coverage of a race-walking competition. Now, here was something I could be good at! I could already walk—certainly, that was half the battle! Strong feet and stocky legs *and* eight years of daily dog walking under my belt! I excitedly purchased the finest running shoe ever created for race walkers and set out on my training program.

Yes, it was a mistake to bring the schnauzers on that pivotal first day. I set off like a shot, swinging my arms like a soldier and striking fear into the hearts of the dogs, as they were sure something was chasing us. After a few blocks, the dogs suspected I had had *way* too much caffeine and executed a strategic full mutiny: paws forward, halt! *This isn't working*, I thought. *I'll just have to get up earlier than 5:15 a.m., walk the dogs first, and then go for my speed walk!* Yes, it lasted three days.

But I wasn't the only hobby seeker in the family. It was my good luck that my husband, Kam, decided to take up golf. After his second lesson, it was clear that he needed the finest Ping golf clubs if he was ever going to be good at the sport. Twelve hundred dollars later, he was toting magnificent clubs that came with their very own bag. Ironically, the bag and clubs became a source of laughter on the fairway. Other golfers would see the golf set and expect this man to, *no doubt*, be one of the finest golfers around. You can imagine their surprise when they watched him swing those beautiful clubs with the grace of a baseball player. After one particularly stunning shot when Kam's ball hit a tree, careened off a golf cart, and almost decapitated a fellow golfer, a man walked up to him and said, "Boy, it's a good thing you have those clubs!" The clubs have stopped swinging and are now buried solemnly in our garage. As a wife, their presence pleases me immensely—for any complaint about my spending can be countered with "Now, where are those Ping golf clubs?" Note to self: there is a difference between buying the best equipment and earning the right to use it.

While my husband immersed himself in work, my hobby quest continued unabated for several years, with early enthusiasm always stuttering to its inevitable, ungracious, and often costly end. Sadly, I found no hidden talents even on the most distant neural synapse. Was there nothing that could provide a complete, albeit temporary, escape from the drudgery of life? For adulthood, now in full swing, often seemed as exciting as bone marrow. Surely there was something to amuse for that precious half hour of every day after chores were done and before utter exhaustion set in? As it turned out, I would have to go full circle and return to where I started before the answer to the dinner-party question appeared clearly before me.

5

La Belle Province

Real answers come to you in the most unexpected places, and sometimes the places that come to you are unexpected. In an ironic swirl of fate, Kam landed a job in Longueuil, Quebec, just a few miles from where I grew up. The location was quite a surprise even to Kam, as he had applied for a job in Alberta, but the company decided they wanted him at their corporate office in Quebec. During the interview, Western Canada became Central Canada, and yes, there's a significant difference—2,310 miles, to be exact. I have to admit, I was a little bug-eyed when I heard the news. "They offered you a job in Quebec? Seriously?" I asked. "You don't even speak French!" Kam had never lived in Quebec, so I wasn't sure how he was going to adapt to being an Anglophone in a predominantly Francophone province. Kam explained that the company was going to send him for eight weeks of intensive French immersion in Jonquière. "Jonquière!" I laughed. "How much French do you think you can learn in eight weeks?"

"Well, a lot of people at the company will speak English too," Kam replied. "I just want to know the basics." Kam's stint living with a French family in Jonquière came and went in a blink of an eye.

I'll never forget his first week on the new job. When Kam arrived home on Friday, I asked him with a mischievous grin, "So, honey, did you speak any French this week?"

He looked at me and said, "Yes, I did. Today I said, *Merci Dieu c'est vendredi.*" (Thank God it's Friday!)

For me, personally, the biggest plus of moving to Quebec was not actually going back to La Belle Province. No; I was more fixated on what the move allowed me to escape. Of course, I realize that any major uprooting involves turbulence. Like being in a washing machine, a move whirls your life around, and you eventually come to a jarring halt when you are ready to dry out and be folded neatly into place again. But this move would be different. In fact, it had an incredibly bright silver lining—a lining so bright it overshadowed any angst of moving to a province known for its bloated bureaucracy, the highest taxes in Canada, and extremely cold winters. You see, because of this move, I would finally say good riddance to my three-hour-a-day life-sucking Toronto commute. I would also be able to quit my mind-numbing job in tax policy—a job that was strangely capable of making me both incredibly bored and anxious, all at the same time. Yes, I would be gloriously unemployed through no fault of my own—it was divine intervention! So, as you can see, there was nothing to worry about. In Quebec, being happily unemployed, I would have lots of extra time to wade through red tape, to wait in doctor's offices for treatment, and to dress for arctic conditions. And at tax time, we always had the option of drowning our sorrows in a bottle of French wine.

Quebec was as I remembered. The roads were still potholed, drivers still aggressive, and curvy, racetrack-like overpasses still standing. I'm convinced that whoever designed Quebec's highways liked to keep things edgy. Snowstorms and ice are just not enough to keep you gripping the wheel. Luckily, we arrived just when the city of Montreal was coming out of an economic lull. Restaurants were crowded, the stores were full of shoppers again, and Quebecers were enjoying festival after festival—Jazz and Just for Laughs being the most famous.

The Notre Dame Basilica was still the pride of old Montreal, eliciting wonder and awe in hordes of tourists (you can spend all day just admiring its stained glass). The basilica was built in Gothic Revival style in 1829 and is an incredibly beautiful example of Church excess. Celine Dion was married there—perhaps that puts it in perspective? But some things had changed in the City. The Montreal Forum, which hosted twenty-four Stanley Cup hockey championships over seven decades, had sadly hung up its skates and been converted to movie theaters, restaurants, and stores. The newer Bell Center had picked up the puck and was now home ice for the beloved Montreal Canadiens hockey team. The Champlain Bridge, which straddles high above the always ominous-looking Saint Lawrence River, must have finally been paid off; I noticed the twenty-five-cent tolls had been torn down. As a child, it had been an exciting moment for me to lean out the car window, fighting high winds, to throw the quarter into the satellite-shaped toll bin. Given Quebec winters and the salting the bridge gets, it's a miracle the behemoth is still standing.

As Mom had predicted, the Frenchification of the province was now complete. English-only signs were gone and replaced with either French-only signs or bilingual signs where the French is strategically made more prominent (as required by law, believe it or not). The most popular hangout for Anglophones now seemed to be the Chapters bookstore on Sainte-Catherine Street. English speakers inundated its coffee shop, leaned against its walls, and camped out in the aisles, blissfully surrounded by their now-precious English-language books. Unfortunately, my memories of Montreal, created so long ago and augmented only by a few scattered visits over the years, were like disjointed sound bites that couldn't quite be pieced together into any sort of meaningful lyric. Mine was a muddied sense of nostalgia.

After we moved into a house in Boucherville, a small town on the south shore, I visited Dad's grave, which is tucked at the back of Paroisse de Saint-Bruno-de-Montarville (the now French Catholic church). A vague sense of direction and half-remembered streets led me to the impressive stone church, its tall spire still reaching for the heavens. It was a crisp, fall day, and a cold wind was blowing the last of the yellow and red leaves around the empty parking lot when I pulled in. As I walked through the cemetery, I read the names on the gravestones—names of the old, the young, mothers and fathers. They were mostly "dearly beloved" with stories told and untold, dreams met and unmet. Some of the monuments were quite tall, with polished stone and detailed engraving, while others were roughly cut, simple, rectangular stones that lay flat against the dying grass. These smaller stones were for the babies, it seemed. When your life has been but a few breaths of time, I guess there is not much to say.

When I finally found Dad's grave, I stood there thinking about how young he had been when he died. There seems no rhyme or reason why some of us live to a ripe, old age and others are so shortchanged. Maybe God takes the good ones first; that seems the only reasonable explanation. I suddenly noticed that other graves had flowers, and I felt sad I hadn't brought any. I listened for a while to the leaves rustling up against the chain link fence at the end of the row and found myself distracted by a fat, gray squirrel two rows over carefully burying nuts in the sacred ground. I stood a little while longer, trying to remember the special moments I had shared with my father. In truth, my well-worn memories were getting dimmer every year, and it saddened me. I wished I could have known him while an adult and not only until I was nine. As I slowly walked back to the car, I glanced up at the old, gnarled trees towering over me. How lucky they were—at least they would be resurrected and leaf out in spring.

Our first winter in Quebec was so cold that by the time Christmas rolled in, our schnauzers were in snowsuits. You know it's cold when your eyelashes frost on morning walks with the dogs. Wearing Sorel boots (which can keep your feet warm even at minus fifteen degrees Fahrenheit) had become an absolute necessity. As the New Year rolled in, icicles around the house were in a state of suspended animation, and the snow, which I knew wouldn't melt till spring, was already several feet deep. On January 5, 1998, however, a very unusual meteorological event occurred—it began to rain freezing rain, and it continued, off and on, for nearly eighty hours.

When the ice storm began, I was running errands, and after leaving a pharmacy, I noticed my windshield had frozen over. I scraped it clean. After about another half hour of shopping at a grocery store, I returned to the car and saw that my windshield was frozen solid once again and had to scrape it again. After a stop at the bank and another round of windshield scraping, I decided that this was really nuts and drove carefully home. The roads actually weren't that bad that morning.

There are a lot of things that don't run efficiently in Quebec, but road salting and sanding is not one of them. No, Quebecers understand winter and how to tackle it. But this was different. By the time I arrived home, our garage door was frozen solid and wouldn't open, so I had to leave the car outside. When Kam returned from work, the ploughs were desperately trying to keep up with the ice accumulation, focusing on the main streets. Consequently, the streets in our small subdivision had turned into mini ice rinks. Luckily, when Kam turned onto our street, he skidded gently into a snowbank, barely missing the neighbor's car.

That night, we sat huddled by our fireplace with the dogs at our feet, listening to the ominous sound of freezing rain pelting the roof. I expected we would lose power, but then the unthinkable happened. Montreal went completely dark. From a bedroom on the second story of our home, we had a good view of the island of Montreal. To look toward a city of 1.7 million people and see the lights off is quite a sight.

The combination of ice rain and additional snowfall over the next few days caused incredible destruction. Sadly, many of Montreal's stately old trees—trees that had for many decades stood strong and determined through fierce Quebec winters—finally succumbed, rather ungracefully, to the sheer weight of ice on their branches. Splitting apart with great booms, pops, and cracks in their last heaving moments, many of those trees, as if to add insult to injury, crashed into the aboveground electricity wires, taking the power out as they fell. Even huge, steel electricity pylons and transformers toppled like matchsticks under the weight of the ice. Yes, innocent rain, with no known demonic tendencies, had transformed to ice and managed, within a few days, to destroy a system of electrical infrastructure that had been built up over decades.

Unlike other natural disasters, which only leave ugliness in their wake, the one redeeming quality of the ice storm was that it turned the landscape into a glorious winter wonder. Photographers worked nonstop to capture the unparalleled beauty of trees, bridges, and whole city streets frosted to icy perfection and glistening under a cold sun. As soon as the ice rain stopped, we managed to pry the garage door open from its bondage by breaking the ice that glued it to the garage floor. My car, having been exposed to the elements, was totally entombed in four inches of ice. Icicles had formed all along the bottom edge of the car, and their points almost hit the ground. It took a good hour, but by tapping gently with a pickaxe, we managed to wrench the car door open and then carefully chiseled a hole in the ice on the windshield so we could see enough to drive the car straight into the garage to thaw. Truly, I was amazed the engine started at all.

We lost power for only four days and were sincerely grateful for the stack of firewood the previous owners of the house had left in the garage. Except for bruising from a nasty fall on an icy sidewalk—a fall that left me wondering if I had broken a hip—I dared not complain. Many people were not as lucky. As a result of the storm, which hit parts of Quebec, Ontario, Nova Scotia, and even northern New York and Maine, thirty-five people lost their lives, and many went without power for weeks.

During the four very quiet, electricity-free days, when the monastic silence prompted much reflection, I realized that, apart from Kam's new work colleagues, the only people we knew in Montreal were Dad's best friend Fritz and his wife Vanda, who still lived in the West End of the City. Unfortunately, driving was so treacherous over the next few months, with a series of blizzards to contend with, that it was early spring before Kam and I were admiring their place settings and tastefully decorated home. My father and Fritz had been so inseparable during life that a string still ties them together in my mind.

It was somehow comforting to me, living once again in Quebec, to visit a friend of my father's. There were so few people by then who had any memory of him. After death, most of us, or at least those whom fame has sidestepped, are so easily forgotten. In fact, generally speaking, we can hope for one or at most two generations before all memory of our time on this planet is completely and utterly obliterated. I'm sure Dad's mind was filled with the same everyday worries that plague us all, but what do those worries matter now?

Rather than make me sad, this reality always reminds me to not take life so seriously. Our lives are such quick blinks in the universe of time. If you don't find joy or even look for it, when will it find you?

In all respects, Fritz is a typical German—intelligent, hardworking, purposeful, and steady. He had spent his entire career at a hardware importing company based in Montreal. Starting at the bottom of the corporate ladder, with determination he moved up each rung to become president of the company. At the time our story unfolds, Fritz had just retired and was still adjusting to the long-expected though sudden change of routine. His wife, Vanda, is a lovely woman from northern Italy who paints beautifully, loves art, and exudes style and grace in everything she does. I like them both immensely. They are also the only people I know who have three pianos in their house, and Fritz plays on all of them. Playing the piano is what gives Fritz joy. It is his answer to the dinner-party question.

On the evening of our visit, after a delightful dinner topped out with herbal tea and shortbread cookies, Fritz sat at a piano, as was his custom, and began to play. Rising from the table, Vanda motioned at us to join her in the living room, saying, "Since he retired, Fritz plays at least two, sometimes three hours a day." I could hear the "Thank God" in her voice, as she too was adjusting to having her husband home full-time.

It had been many years since I had heard Fritz play. As I sat there listening to one amazing rendition of classical music after another, I couldn't contain myself. "Fritz!" I exclaimed, "You play so wonderfully! You should play with an orchestra or in public. I'm sure people would love to hear you play!"

He thanked me for the compliments but then said to me in his considered way, "But Dagny, I don't play for others. I play because I love to play. I don't need to be in public or have other people tell me I'm good or bad. I just play." And with that, he dove into a magnificent Rachmaninoff concerto.

I couldn't believe that most of the time, the only person who ever hears Fritz play is his wife of forty years. But then I thought about it: *this* is what a hobby should be—not egocentric, not competitive, not praise seeking. At that very moment, the next thing that popped into my head was: *What if I took up riding again? What if I rode just for the fun of it? No competitions, no ego, just ride?* Mysteriously, that thought then whispered through the universe like a butterfly flapping its wings.

The very next morning, quite out of the blue, I received a call from a woman named Catherine whom I had met recently at a company dinner party. I had liked her instantly, and we were sure to be best buddies—she was smart, funny, and apparently the only English speaker within a twenty-mile radius of our home. When she called that morning, after the usual hellos and how-are-yous, she suddenly asked, "Hey, do you want to take a horseback riding lesson with me? There is going to be a trail ride at the company picnic, and I don't want to make a fool of myself. Why don't we go together? It'll be fun!" I stood there quietly for a while, just holding the phone—the universe had obviously responded, and it was patently clear that the sign said, "You must ride again!"

"OK, I'll go," I replied tentatively and promised to make the arrangements. After hanging up the phone, I took off like a shot and began rummaging excitedly through kitchen drawers, looking for the French-English dictionary. When I finally found it wedged beside the kitchen spices, I pulled it out, throwing it on the counter. *So, how does one say stable in French? OK:* écurie. Step two was a search through the French-language phone book that came with the house, and *voilà, une écurie!* Riding instruction was within five miles! After an awkward telephone conversation that left me hoping the barn owner understood we wanted to ride *les chevaux* and that I didn't want a haircut (that would be *les cheveux*), everything was set. Nothing left to do but skip joyously around the house, dusting everything in sight.

A few days later, Catherine and I were standing in front of the much-anticipated *écurie*, which turned out to be a simple, apparently homemade barn surrounded by thick masses of fir trees. I wasn't sure if the trees were to protect the barn from winter winds or to hold it up. The horses were housed in dark stalls with very small windows. Luckily, the top halves of the stall doors were open, so the horses could at least peer up and down the dark aisle to see sunlight shining brightly outside.

The instructor, Monique, was a young twentysomething. She was quite a pretty girl, with beautiful green eyes. Her shiny, black hair was cut in a stylish bob, and she was wearing a black Western horse shirt and tight blue jeans. I could tell having English clients was a novelty, and she was a little shy to speak with us at first. "So, Danny, you say you ride, no?" asked Monique. (Yes, it's unfortunate, but in French, my name takes on a slightly masculine flair.)

"Yes," I replied, smiling. "I rode when I was young."

"And how many years before?"

"It's been eighteen years since I was on a horse."

"Ah, *bien*...and *vous*, Catherine?"

"I've never ridden before," replied Catherine.

"OK, then. Danny, you ride first, and we see, yes?"

Monique had already tacked up what looked like a *very* mellow school horse for me to ride. Truthfully, my initial impression was that the horse was in a coma. My steed was a stocky-looking, nondescript horse that had been left standing on one crosstie in the barn aisle. He was tied rather loosely and stood with his nose almost to his knees. From my angle, it appeared he was snoring. Monique noticed my stare and said, "Don't worree, he's *fatigué* because of two *leçons* before you. In de riding, everything OK, *il est très bon.*" As it turned out, the horse was indeed a power napper, and he did perk up nicely in the ring.

Climbing up into a saddle again was wonderful, but I didn't have time to dilly-dally. After helping me adjust the stirrups, Monique immediately put me through the paces. It wasn't long before I learned that in French, *le trot assis* means "sitting trot," *le trot enlevé* means "posting trot," and *un petit galop* means "to canter." The latter should not be literally translated as a *little gallop* around the ring! Monique did seem shocked when I took off at a hand gallop. All in all, considering the eighteen-year hiatus, I rode pretty well. The walk seemed to come naturally enough, and I remembered the up-and-down motion of the posting trot. The gallop was, in hindsight, too fast, and I went veering around the ring like a motorcyclist, leaning dramatically to the inside, but I didn't fall off, and I don't think I stopped smiling for a second. After watching me for a while, Monique said, "You not beginner, 'ow you say? *Intermédiaire.* You have the legs steady." Well, steady legs sounded encouraging. My legs were indeed short, little tree trunks, and that probably helped them be so steady. Of course, instructors are always most generous with their compliments during that crucial first lesson when they reel you in!

While Catherine had her turn on the horse, I walked up and down the barn aisle, petting all the soft noses and whispering sweet nothings into the flickering, fuzzy ears of any horse willing to listen. What struck me most about the experience that day were the smells of the barn I remembered and loved so well: of horses and hay, leather and shavings, grain and liniment. Like an addict who reaches for a drug after a lengthy withdrawal, I knew I was hooked, line and sinker. The magic of Equus once again had me tight in its grasp.

For Catherine, the barn experience was equally momentous but for different reasons. Halfway through her lesson, she turned beet red, swelled up like a beach ball, and broke out into hives. A visit to the emergency room and a few epinephrine shots later confirmed a pretty serious horse allergy. Who would have thought! I had heard of people being allergic to dogs and cats, but I didn't know people could be allergic to horses. Certainly, there was no trail riding in Catherine's future. I, on the other hand, finally had a superb answer to the dinner-party question: horseback riding. It seemed like a splendid choice, suggesting a love of animals and courage. And, as it turned out, a good dose of courage was going to be needed.

6

Returning to Center

"I thought you said Notre Dame East crossed Haig Street," Kam said.

"Well, I thought it did," I replied tentatively, trying to hide the doubt in my voice. "Notre Dame should be coming up soon," I added. As we continued passing street after street, I became increasingly anxious that we were indeed lost. We still didn't know the Island of Montreal that well, and unfortunately we were living in the paleo-iPhone age, without a shiny, blue dot to guide us.

After about ten more minutes of driving, I could feel the tension in the car rise—as happens with many couples when trapped in a car together, circling city blocks with no obvious path to their destination. Of course, our circling was made more pronounced by Kam's strong tendency to turn right at intersections when lost. Like most men, Kam preferred to solve his own problems, and stopping to ask for directions was out of the question. "After all," he explained, "you just don't want people to know you're lost, especially in a neighborhood like this." I had to admit, the neighborhood was a little questionable and featured an odd mix of commercial buildings, small factories, graffiti-covered apartment buildings, rundown homes, cute bungalows, and new construction. Yes, there are always the optimists willing to wedge new construction between decrepit teardowns, no matter how odd it looks.

This East End of Montreal certainly couldn't hold a candle to Montreal's more elegant West End, where stately old mansions, museums, leafy bike trails, and pleasant public parks hold sway. Historically, the English have lived in the West End of Montreal while the French have lived in the East End of the island. Looking around me that day, I began to think, *Maybe that is why the French are always so miffed at us English.* It did seem we had a monopoly on the better side of the tracks.

Thankfully, in the far distance, I finally saw the words *Notre Dame E.* written on the next street sign. With great confidence, I said, "Hon, turn right at the next street." As we turned right, I spotted the sign for Sellerie Lemay (Lemay Saddle Shop) and sighed an inner *Thank goodness!* Surprisingly, the boxy, redbrick building with its metal-framed glass door and windows looked more like an old, Italian bakery than a horse-tack shop. The glass on the front door of the store was so plastered with ads that I couldn't get a glimpse of the interior. As I swung the door open, I said a quick prayer, hoping the store was going to be worth our one-hour battle through Pont LaFontaine traffic and this somewhat daring visit to the east side of town.

With one step into the shop, however, I was overpowered by the strong smell of new leather saddles and bridles—yes, this was the all-too-familiar *parfum de chevaux*. The shop was indeed a horse-lover's mecca, filled to the rafters with saddles, bridles, English and Western riding boots, breeches, helmets, gloves, brushes, horse vitamins, "how-to-ride" books, horsey greeting cards, horse jewelry, and all things whinny. Walking reverently up and down each aisle, I recognized many tools of the horse trade and suddenly appreciated all the pony-club seminars I had attended as a child. Arriving at the back wall of the shop, I noticed Breyer model-horse statues lining a top shelf. I remembered seeing them in tack shops twenty years earlier, and it was somehow comforting to know the company was still making them. Interesting enough, the Breyer Molding Company, as it was originally called, got its start in Chicago in 1950 when it manufactured a model-horse statue to adorn a mantelpiece clock—however, once the item was on display, people started calling the company, wanting to know if they could buy the horse without the clock part—certainly an interesting start to a model-horse business empire!

Stopping at some bridles, I was delicately running a leather rein through my fingers when I was suddenly startled by a salesperson. *"Puis-je vous aider?"* (Can I help you?)

"Oui, merci, nous voudrions..." (Yes, thank you, we would like...) I explained to the salesperson in my very best French that my husband and I were there to buy riding clothes. As soon as the salesperson heard me speak French, she immediately switched to English—Montreal language etiquette in action.

Yes, it was unfortunate, but after eight years of formal language instruction, including even a few university-level classes, it was apparent to everyone after I uttered even only one or two words that I am not a Francophone. Since moving to Quebec, I was determined to improve my French and practice at every opportunity, so a salesperson's switch to English was always disconcerting. A few days earlier, at a Réno-Dépôt store, I pretended I hadn't noticed the salesperson's switch to English and just kept rambling on in French. This tactic, however, backfired, as rather than switch back to French, the salesperson continued on in English. We then had the ultimate bilingual conversation, with the French salesperson awkwardly asking me questions in English and me replying in my equally awkward, high-pitched French. I mention higher pitch because for some reason, speaking French always raises my voice at least one octave. Yes, apparently my French voice has the appeal of a snooty French poodle. *Hmmm...maybe that's it. Maybe I speak the language brilliantly, and the salespeople switch to English because they don't like the sound of my French voice?*

On that day, however, having just endured the stress of driving around town completely lost, I decided that speaking English was just the thing I needed. As the young lady led us to the clothing section of the store, I wanted to pinch myself. Not only would I soon be riding again, but also, I had brilliantly managed to convince my husband to take up the sport. "Hon, you've been wanting to try a new hobby since you gave up on golf. Why not try riding? It would be something we could do together!" In truth, Kam had no real interest in riding, and his "Sure, I'll take riding lessons with you" had been filled with the same reluctance I hear when I excitedly run up to him with a chick flick at the video store. But I was willing to sweep any hesitation on his part under the rug, for I was sure that once he was formally introduced to horses, they would weave their magic and capture his heart.

As Kam and I surveyed the riding-boot aisle, I stopped to examine some rubber boots on a shelf. "You don't want to buy those," Kam said. "Get yourself a good pair of real leather boots. You might also want to get a warm pair for the winter."

"Really?" I replied with a grin, and stepping up onto my tiptoes, I gave Kam a tender kiss on the cheek. He looked at me a little puzzled, not quite understanding my sincere appreciation. Unless you've experienced it, it is hard to imagine the shooting pain that runs through your feet and legs when you dismount from a horse with frozen toes. As a child, I distinctly remember during the depths of a Quebec winter when I looked at the arena floor just prior to dismounts, thinking, *Geez, Louise, this is going to hurt!*

Yes, things were going to be different now. Imagine, fur-lined riding boots! And the horse world was enjoying a few brilliant technical advancements as well. Someone had invented little sachets called HotHands that you could stuff into the palms of your riding gloves to keep your hands toasty. I grabbed a few as we approached the cash register. We were now ready for the Quebec winter and the dreaded unheated horse barn. There would be no losing of extremities to frostbite.

Within a week, Kam and I had enrolled in riding lessons. "Hon, our first lesson is this Saturday."

"This Saturday?" he replied. "That was fast."

"Well, you said *you* wanted to take riding lessons," I said with emphasis as if simply trying to assist him with his new hobby. Kam quickly realized that when it came to horses and all things horse related, I could be incredibly efficient. Bills could pile up, ironing could sit wrinkled, the fridge might be empty, but ask me to schedule a riding lesson or a trail ride, and I could demonstrate Martha Stewart–like organization skills.

At first, I tried to appear nonchalant about getting back into riding. Come lesson day, however, with excitement and anxiety mixed in equal parts, the enthusiasm took on a different tone. "Hurry up, we're going to be late! We have to arrive at least a half hour early to groom the horses! Why do you always take so long to get ready? Come on!" Berating my husband prior to our "fun" riding lesson probably wasn't the best tactic to take on my part, but we'll chalk that up to marital inexperience.

Kam and I arrived at our first lesson looking like we had stepped out of an equestrian fashion magazine. Even our instructor, Monique, stopped to admire our clean attire and smiled. "Well, you are very *préparé*!" As she politely showed us around the facility, I noticed a row of tattered, cobweb-covered riding helmets on the wall and was grateful for the clean, black-velvet helmet I was protectively holding against my chest.

As I suspected it would, my honeymoon with Monique ended quickly. Once she felt sufficiently at ease with me, the real teaching began. It turned out her initial assessment of my riding skill was completely wrong, and suddenly, there was a lot I needed to change. First, Monique had to address the fetal position I was riding in. Apparently, I would sit with my upper body slanted forward toward the horse's ears. This, I was told, was just a natural reaction because I feared letting go and sitting up straight. Following her advice to sit up straighter, I then developed the dreaded "chair seat." This is when you sit on the saddle like you are sitting in a La-Z-Boy chair with your feet sticking out in front of you. I had, apparently, overcorrected. The ideal is to be centered on the horse's back, keeping your ears aligned with your hips and ankles, and without either arching your back or rounding your shoulders. Let me assure you, this is easier said than done.

To further complicate matters, my mind and body seemed stuck on different radio frequencies—the body was set on AM while the mind was on FM, and there was no meaningful transmission between the two. For example, after being given instruction to perform two circles at a sitting trot and cross the arena on the diagonal, all while remembering to look up and keep my heels down, I would head out focused totally on the last part of the instruction, keeping my heels down and head up but forgetting in which direction or on what diagonal I was supposed to go. Even the horse could sense my confusion, as it would sometimes trot straight toward a wall and on approach seem to yell up to me, "Well, are we going left or right, lady? *Left or right?*" Progress continued, turtlelike, for several months.

Over time, I became quite conscious of the fact that Kam was taking to riding like a fish to water. In just a few lessons, he seemed to have mastered the basics and had a natural seat. I remember during one lesson, I was in the center of the arena when the instructor asked Kam to take his horse and canter around the ring for the first time. Expecting a mishap, I kept my eyes glued to the ground. When I heard the instructor's praise, I looked up, only to see Kam confidently circling the ring. No, I wasn't at all jealous of his ability, just royally peeved—*I can't believe he has more natural talent for riding than I do! I know he has longer legs and a better-proportioned body, but gee whiz, I've taken lessons for years!* At that very moment, I had a cruel flashback to our high-school days when I would study for weeks for an exam and barely eke out a 75 out of 100 while Kam wouldn't study at all and come out of the exam with a 102 out of 100 (the extra two being bonus points). I swallowed my pride back then, but now this! As I watched him canter around the ring effortlessly, I rolled my eyes and muttered "Darn it!" under my breath.

When he returned to the center of the arena, Kam was all smiles, and reaching down to pet his horse, he said, "Hey, that was fun! Easier than I thought it would be."

"Holy crow, hon," I said, smiling and shaking my head. "Is there nothing you aren't good at? Leave me some bread crumbs, won't you?"

As the months passed, I sensed a difference between my pre- and postlesson emotional states. I began each lesson with the optimism of a cheerleader but ended with the seriousness of a quarterback who had fumbled the ball. My usual self-talk on leaving the barn and getting back into my car was: *Dagny, it is just a hobby. Don't be so serious about it. You are riding for your own pleasure, remember? Relax, enjoy, have fun. You will get better...eventually...hopefully.*

As time went by, Kam rode less, and I rode more. Ironic, don't you think? My husband, with his natural talent to excel at riding, wasn't that interested in taking lessons, while I, still searching for even a toothpick of improvement, was determined to take lessons week after week, so help me God. As Kam explained, "Dagny, I love horses, and they are really, really special creatures, but I just don't like the lesson part and all that going in circles." Having spent my entire childhood circling on horses, the idea of going straight or really going anywhere on horseback hadn't even occurred to me. I don't know if it was bullheadedness on my part or just a pure, heroinlike addiction to horses, but I wasn't going to throw in the reins.

After being back in the saddle for about a year, I realized that to do something without a specific goal is often viewed by others as utterly bizarre. For example, one day, a fellow rider asked me, "So, what type of riding do you do?"

I replied, a bit perplexed, "Ah, I don't know. General riding?"

"No," she replied with a laugh, "I mean, what do you want to do? Do you want to compete in Western or English classes? Show jumping? Three-day eventing? Dressage? Roping? Cutting? What are your goals?" At that point, I didn't even quite understand what roping or cutting were (and I was quite suspicious of the words themselves), but I knew what she meant. She was just one of many people (like friends, family members, and colleagues) who just wanted to know *why* I was riding. Fair enough; I sometimes wondered myself—why was I taking all these lessons? Would true happiness come with a successfully executed side pass? Perhaps I would be overcome with bliss if I could actually perform a flying lead change or figure out where the horse's feet are supposed to be during a shoulder-in. I was sure I would never set foot in a show ring again.

My official explanation, which I regularly offered up at dinner parties or whenever anyone asked, was that "At my age, I just don't care about winning ribbons." I always spoke these words in a haughty tone as if to imply that competing for accolades or any such trifle was just beneath me. Truthfully? I hadn't wrestled my ego to the ground and couldn't bear the embarrassment of still coming in dead last.

My mind was also plagued by dreamlike images of me entering a show ring on an assigned school horse, trying to ride through a full-blown equine temper tantrum and being ungraciously bucked off in front of a large audience. You see, I just don't have the courage of a figure skater. Yes, figure skaters are my heroes. They are willing to perform in front of a large audience with all eyes staring just at them and take the risk of falling right on their asses! Sometimes they fall several times during just one performance, yet they forge ahead undaunted, with the determination of a Roman warrior to the bitter end. They don't even have a horse to blame for their errors. Now, that takes guts. No, I'm not figure-skater material, and I certainly wasn't going to embarrass myself on the horse-show circuit.

As time passed, however, I did consider my riding options. Show jumping and three-day eventing (which also involves jumping) were definitely out of the question. Of equestrian sports, jumping is the most dangerous. In fact, many people don't realize this, but equestrian jumping is one of *the* most dangerous sports in the world—yes, it's right up there with rugby and heli-skiing. Also, having spent my entire childhood riding English style, I didn't think I could make the switch to Western riding. Heck, I hadn't yet mastered English riding, and I didn't want to become even more confused.

Although dressage riders with their black riding outfits and tall, black hats always look a bit constipated to me, it is hard not to admire the way their magnificent horses seem to respond to their every thought—so I decided to give dressage a try. I wouldn't compete, *of course*. I would just try to learn how to ride like a dressage rider but without the top hat and coat. Apparently, dressage is becoming increasingly popular with middle-aged women who are getting back into riding but are worried about the dangers of equestrian jumping. It seemed I fit the demographic perfectly.

No sooner had I settled on my new riding goal than my husband decided we were moving to another country. Yes, it was a bit of a shock to my system. In fact, I distinctly remember breaking into a sudden fit of coughing when he told me. After all, we had only taken root in Montreal three years prior. His company was transferring him to their US headquarters, and we were destined for Hartford, Connecticut. Yes, money often makes the world go round, and sometimes it pulls you in an unexpected direction. Regular paychecks are just so addictive. Not that I was terribly sad to leave Quebec, but I had grown to appreciate some of its finer points. Montreal's restaurant scene is just delicious, its art galleries always brimming with hushed excitement, and its cultural events too many to number. And after some strategic investments in snowsuits and wool everything, one can actually begin to enjoy winter.

For example, on one vacation, we traveled with a group of friends just north of Quebec City to cross-country ski, snowmobile, and dogsled all in the same week. When your vacation involves sleeping in a teepee and learning how to tap a maple tree for maple syrup, you just start to feel very Canadian. Though I must admit, for me personally, cross-country skiing involves too much falling over onto one's side and unladylike splaying of legs. Snowmobiling is like riding a very fast, noisy lawnmower for hours on end, disturbing any peace that nature provides, and it can also leave you with a throbbing headache. Dogsledding, however, was hysterical.

Given that many readers may never have had the opportunity to step astride the footboards of a dogsled, let me take you back to that day when we were first introduced to this Canadian Inuit tradition. To set the tone, our guide told us in utmost seriousness that the most important thing about dogsledding was to not let go of the sled. "The dogs are not like a motorboat. They won't turn round to pick you up if you fall but likely keep running for mile after mile. Second, you should try to keep a good distance between dog teams so the dogs don't get tangled together and start fighting. Three, try not to hit trees or big boulders with the sled, and four, just put your weight on the claw brake when you want to slow down."

"What if we want to speed up?" Kam asked.

"Speed won't be your problem. Not with these dogs," the guide replied with a smirk.

Our group was then driven to an area where three teams of huskies were harnessed and waiting for us. As soon as the guide approached the sleds, the dogs started barking excitedly and lunging wildly against their harnesses. If the sleds hadn't been solidly staked, the dogs, like coiled springs, would have taken off without us. I jumped into the basket of one of the sleds and settled under a nice, warm blanket while Kam took to the rails. After a jolting, slightly chaotic start, we were bombing down narrow, snow-packed trails through thick stands of birch and maple trees. Once running, the dogs settled down, and all we could hear as we traveled over frozen lakes and forests was the crunch of the sled rails against the snow and the excited panting of the dogs as they happily filled their lungs with the cold air of winter.

As I sat comfortably in the basket, I thought, *Oh, this is so much nicer than snowmobiling!* Then it happened. One of the dogs tried to slow down as he arched his back to take a dump. The poor thing half ran and half pooped as the sled continued forward. The poop then traveled directly under the sled below me, and Kam and I were hit with the worst poop smell you can imagine. Screeching with laughter, we continued on, but then another dog decided it was time to go, and Kam started yelling, "Get ready, it's coming at you!" I covered my mouth and nose with the blanket and was just dying with laughter as yet another poop bomb traveled toward me and then under the sled.

A third dog joined the fray with a diarrhea load, and I just about peed my pants laughing. After this dog finished, I yelled at the team, "So, are we done yet?" The dogs settled back into their running, apparently the morning's breakfast having been dealt with.

Kam looked so comfortable driving the sled that at the first rest stop, I insisted I try driving. We exchanged places and all started well, but we started going faster than I wanted, so I jumped onto the claw brake. Nothing happened. I jumped onto the brake again, but the sled didn't slow. My weight wasn't enough to dig the clamps into the icy snow, and we started traveling faster and faster. Scared, I twisted my body to yell at the team behind me that I couldn't brake, and in doing so, I put too much weight onto one rail and turned the sled right onto its side. Kam, pitched sideways but still in the basket, was trying to right the sled with his weight while I had lost all footing and was holding onto the sled with only one arm, being dragged through the snow like an anchor. The lead team heard our shouts and stopped their dogs, so our dogs came to a stop as well. When the guide ran up to me, I was covered head to foot in snow and the sled was still lying on its side, but I had managed to keep a death grip with one arm onto the rail. He leaned over me with a look of concern on his face, the bright blue sky haloed around him. "Are you OK?" he asked.

I looked up at him with a big smile and said, "Hey, I didn't let go of the sled!"

"No, you didn't! You're a true Canadian now," he replied as he grabbed my hand and helped me back onto my feet.

Kam, having righted the sled, looked at me, laughing and shaking his head. "I think it might be a better idea if I drive." I jumped back into the basket and decided that being warm under a blanket and enjoying the scenery fly by was a good thing.

To add to the tourist dogsledding experience, that night, eight of us slept on the floor of a real teepee in sleeping bags. The teepee had been slightly modernized with a wood stove that had a long metal pipe that shot up and out the center of the teepee, venting to the outside. Given it was minus twenty degrees that night, I'm glad we weren't historical purists, as

I'm sure real Indians didn't enjoy the warmth of a metal wood stove.

The guide stoked the stove with dry wood before we all snuggled into our sleeping bags for the night. I watched the golden, flickering light cast soft shadows onto the cream-colored teepee hide until falling asleep. About 1:00 a.m., Kam and I woke to the sound of one husky barking. All the other dogs were quiet, but this one dog just wouldn't shut up. Nobody else in the teepee seemed to be bothered by the barking, but we lay there awake, hoping the dog would stop. After about ten minutes of the barking, Kam rolled over toward me in his sleeping bag and whispered, "I'm going to kill that dog!" Twenty minutes later, the dog still hadn't stopped barking. Kam unzipped his sleeping bag, and getting up, said, "That's it!"

Trying not to wake the others, I whispered, "What do you think you're doing? You can't beat the dog! Don't go outside!" Kam didn't listen to me, and quietly putting on his jacket, he unzipped the teepee door flap and left.

A few minutes later, the dog stopped barking. I heard the teepee door being unzipped again, and there was Kam, holding a husky firmly by the collar. He brought the dog inside and made him lie down beside my sleeping bag. The dog was young and, overwhelmed by the privilege of joining the humans, lay still and quiet. Once Kam was back in his sleeping bag, the dog huddled a little closer to him and laid his head appreciatively on Kam's legs. All three of us slumbered back into a peaceful sleep. There are not too many places in North America where you can spend a cold winter night sleeping in a teepee with a husky dog. As it turned out, Quebec does have its fair share of pluses, and it was with oddly mixed feelings that I prepared for our new life in the United States of America.

Although the move was a logistical challenge, living in Connecticut turned out to be as easy as pie. First, I had to adapt to my new, all-English environment. Having lived in an all-French neighborhood in Quebec, I had grown accustomed to the daily challenge of communicating in French. My bilingual dictionary had sat by the phone that whole time and came in handy when I had to order something in French over the phone, like pizza (*What is the word for* pepperoni?) gutter cleaning (*How do you say* gutter?) or cable repair (*How on earth do I explain that the cable box is malfunctioning?*) Now that I was in Connecticut, ordering everything in English seemed absolutely effortless.

Americans also offer superb customer service—something that is very hit or miss in Quebec. Soon after arriving in Connecticut, I became convinced that Americans are the most organized people on the planet. In Quebec, I would wait in a doctor's office for *hours* before the doctor would see me. In Connecticut, I could barely finish a single paragraph of a trashy magazine before the nurse would efficiently call me in to see the doctor. And Connecticut roads! Even in remote, wooded areas outside of the main cities, the state of Connecticut has somehow managed to build smooth roads that roll effortlessly over their leafy, treed hills. Unless you've survived a car-swallowing Montreal pothole or been subjected to Quebec's infrastructure, you really can't appreciate the difference.

Connecticut's fall foliage is also truly spectacular, with an incredible variety in leaf color—from the deepest reds to the palest of yellows. During its hot, humid summers, farmers' markets welcome Saturday mornings with fresh, organic produce and cut flowers. At these local events, niche companies ply the freshest of cheeses, honey, herbs, and apparently happily grown cows and chickens. As if to add further charm, elegant New England mansions dot Connecticut's rolling hills. These stately homes, so graciously landscaped with flowering dogwoods, mountain laurel, and well-trimmed boxwood, exude a certain pride and sophistication. Even the roses and ivy are delighted by the architectural charms of these old buildings, as they seem determined to hug every pillar. When I realized Mark Twain wrote some of his best-loved novels while living in Hartford, I decided that was it—Connecticut was just fine by me.

It took me six months to really settle into my new country. There was the unpacking and organizing of the house to complete. I then applied for my Connecticut driver's license and patiently waited for my green card. It's a good thing I have a lot of patience, as it took two years to get the precious card. And when it did come in, I was oddly disappointed that it wasn't really green!

Of course, while I waited for the privilege of being gainfully employed, there were other things to excite me. I learned that in Connecticut, freezing rain is a regular occurrence and, after performing a few 360s in my little Toyota, I decided to avoid leaving the premises whenever it was forecast. And, being the neurotic person that I am, I became a walking encyclopedia on Lyme disease (deer and ticks being very prevalent in the state). I started wearing socks over my pant legs whenever I came within ten feet of a shrub and eventually learned how to pull the little buggers out of the dogs.

Of course, nothing can ever compare to 9/11, the day the Twin Towers fell in New York. Within moments of the first strike, my mother rang me on the phone, and it took some time to reassure her that Connecticut is a fair distance away from downtown Manhattan. "Yes, Mom, I promise. I will be careful and report anything suspicious to the police." Watching the media coverage of planes crashing into the World Trade Center was surreal—like reality TV gone awry. We didn't really know what to make of it all. But it was somewhat comforting to think that, if we knocked politely at the border, Canada would take us back and let us hide under its flag.

When I was finally legally allowed to work, I managed to get myself a job at a local translation agency. My knowledge of French, which had improved after three years of forced immersion in Quebec, finally came in handy. I did, after all, know the word for *gutters*. As soon as life returned to that normal rhythm that many of us are accustomed to—get up, go to work, return from work, make dinner, clean house, watch a half hour of TV, and collapse into bed—I began to pine for horses once again and looked for a new riding stable. Since I had already entertained the hope that I would one day reach the highest levels of dressage—the elegantly named Prix St. Georges—only a stable that focused on dressage would do. Unfortunately, the dressage barn I found was more than an hour-and-a-half drive from the house. At that distance, I decided to limit my riding lessons to once a month. I realized I wouldn't make much progress, but at least I could keep my feet in the stirrups.

My new instructor was another twentysomething named Amanda. How did these women manage to become instructors at such a young age? At our first meeting, I had to admit, however, she certainly looked the part. Amanda was stylishly dressed in Dover catalog apparel. Her long, brown hair was tied back in a ponytail, and she looked like a catalog model herself. Her leather boots were immaculately polished, and she had the tall, thin frame typical of dressage riders. (Yes. You may not have realized this, but dressage riders apparently think big is better and have a strong preference for *enormous* horses. The result? Tall riders seem to have the upper hand. Truly, at five foot two, I really don't know what possessed me to choose dressage!) When I booked my first lesson, I was told that Amanda was riding third-level dressage, and although I wasn't quite sure what that meant, it sounded impressive.

On lesson days, during the long drive to the barn, I always had butterflies in my stomach as I wondered which horse I would be assigned to ride. One of my favorite parts of the whole experience, believe it or not, was just after arriving in the barn's driveway. I would jump into the backseat of the car to put my riding boots and half chaps on. Pulling on my boots and wrapping those chaps around my stocky calves made me feel like a horse-crazy kid again. Of course, I would then stand up and do a few much-needed stretches because, after all, I wasn't fifteen anymore.

I always arrived extra early to groom my assigned mount. After forty-five minutes of body brushing, mane combing, and hoof picking, the school horse would invariably start rolling its eyes, saying, "Enough already, you clean freak!" Much to my annoyance, Amanda spent so much time chatting with other barn people that my lesson was often late. Sometimes, even halfway through the class, she would spot someone on the side of the arena and have a quick chat with him or her. All I could think was, *Lady, I'm spending forty-five dollars an hour for this lesson, so get your third-level behind over here to help me!* Of course, some things are never said out loud.

As time went by, I did gain a better understanding of some of the objectives of dressage and some of the terms. For example, in dressage, you try to keep the horse's head essentially down or arched so he can round his back and better carry the weight of the rider. This is why dressage horses often seem like they are oddly fixated on the ground in front of them. Allowing your horse to trot around the ring with his nose in the air is really a faux pas. I was really mystified by the term *poll* until I learned it is the spot on top of the horse's head, between its ears. I also realized that being on the forehand has nothing to do with tennis but rather means the horse is carrying too much of his weight on his front legs. Despite learning these important tidbits of information, my actual riding skills stayed rather mediocre. I gave Amanda a good year to see what I could learn from her, but I knew we weren't really clicking and eventually began thinking about trying to find another barn and instructor. Interesting enough, it turned out my new stable was going to be a little farther away.

There is a saying that women marry their fathers; well, apparently, I married my mother. Perhaps I have the words "highly adaptable" written on my forehead. Or maybe it says, "Lots of moving experience, can be bribed into relocation, will avoid conflict at all cost." Whatever the reason, like my childhood with my mother, my life with my husband seems to be peppered with regular visits by Allied Van Lines. As soon as I get settled, start to make friends, start to know my way around, or optimistically plant a few trees in my new backyard, my life is wrenched out from under me, and I'm expected to enjoy the thrill of our new adventure.

This time, the "adventure" would be in Washington State, where my husband had accepted a new job with a new company. We had lived in Connecticut for only four years. Upon hearing this *oh, so joyful* news, I immediately opened my National Geographic atlas to find out where Washington State was. After all, I was a Canadian and could be forgiven for not knowing where all fifty states are. I quickly discovered that Washington State is not on the East Coast; that is Washington, DC. No, Washington State is clear across the country from Connecticut! Kam, sensing my shock and disappointment at the prospect of yet another move to a galaxy far, far away, then made the following solemn bribe: "I promise that in Washington State, you can take riding lessons once a week!" Safe with the knowledge that at least I could keep my riding going, I began to accept the new geography. Little did I know that in my riding quest, I would soon hit rock bottom.

7

In Washington State with No Right Turns

"**M**om just dropped the phone! She's crying."

Kam looked at me and smiled. He knew they were tears of joy. I had just phoned my mother to tell her we were moving to Washington State and would be living within a couple of hours' drive from her home in Chilliwack, British Columbia. She couldn't believe her ears that her daughter was going to be living only a short, international border crossing away. Mom had moved to British Columbia a few years earlier to live closer to my brother, Earl. Oh, it wasn't that she loved him more than she loved me or that the mild Vancouver weather had enticed her to move out west. No, the real reason for the move was that Earl had given her two grandchildren, whereas I had only given her two miniature schnauzers. Grandchildren trump dogs, no matter how fluffy.

I waited a good long time on the phone, as mother was now both coughing and crying from excitement. I was starting to get a bit worried lest I might need to send an ambulance, but she finally picked up the phone and sputtered, "I just can't believe it. Oh my God, you've made me so happy!" and burst into another round of tears. Eventually, I heard her take a deep breath and regain her composure. She picked up the phone a third time and said with the gravest of concern, "What about Bear?" Mom knew that my number-one worry would be how I was going to get my eleven-year-old dog, Bear, from Connecticut to Washington State. I had become especially attached to Bear since his brother Teddy had passed away a few years earlier. Unfortunately, Bear had a serious case of separation anxiety and would freak out whenever I left him alone in the house for even a few hours. I too suffered from this same mental condition, as whenever I was away from Bear (even for a few hours), a deep wad of anxiety would take hold in the pit of my stomach. Yes, I admit I may have played a small role in Bear's problem. I regularly lavished the dog with hugs and kisses, took him on long walks every day, brushed and combed his gray fur and beard to perfection, never missed our daily playtime, kept the pantry well stocked with his favorite doggy treats, and basically served his every need. Now, what dog wouldn't get attached to that? My mother (God love her) immediately offered to drive the dog across the United States for me. I know if I had said yes, she would have done it, but I didn't want my sixty-seven-year-old mother driving that distance. No; flying was the most efficient way to get him from point A to point B.

A few days later, I sat myself down on the couch with Bear at my side and went into overdrive, calling every airline to see if any of them would allow me to take him in the passenger area. Unfortunately, Bear was just a tad too big to be shoved under a seat. In desperation, I even called Air France, having heard that they were especially dog friendly. "Is there any chance that Air France flies from New York to Seattle?" I asked with only the feeblest of hope.

"No, madam," replied the agent with a little snicker. "We do fly from New York to Paris, though."

"Oh. Thanks, anyway," I replied, hanging up the phone. "I'm sorry, Bear, but you're going to have to go cargo!"

At that very moment, Bear placed his head on my leg and looked up at me with his sweet, brown eyes as if to say, "I know you tried, Mommy."

Kam, being the most dedicated employee ever, started working at his new job prior to moving day. This meant I would have to stay back in Connecticut to handle all the arrangements and supervise the packing. Of course, having had tremendous moving experience, I felt up to the task.

Don't worry, honey, I'll be fine. You just concentrate on your work. After the house was emptied and all our belongings and my car were now safe in the care of Allied Van Lines, Bear and I sat alone on the front porch—it was just he and I, a large dog crate, and a small suitcase. The house was now an empty shell waiting for its new owners and a new set of dreams to arrive.

My boss's son, Francesco, had offered to drive Bear and me to a hotel near JFK Airport, and I knew he would arrive shortly. It was a cool day in March, and pulling my jacket around me a little tighter, I thought about the fact that spring would be arriving soon. In the backyard of the house was a rose garden I had planted the year before that I would never see bloom. And at the side of the house was a bald patch of land that I had covered with wildflower seed. I wondered if the seeds would grow. I guess we hadn't really taken root in Connecticut, only sprinkled a few seeds.

I sat there stroking Bear's soft, gray fur, nostalgically thinking about the past and wondering about the future. The dog seemed to understand that this was a momentous occasion, and he sat beside me on the porch as still as a statue, his sturdy little schnauzer body somehow grounding him. "Well, Bear," I said, looking into his dark-brown eyes, "when I die, at least no one will say I had a boring life! And for a dog, you are pretty well traveled yourself!"

When I finally saw Francesco's car in the distance, I got up to meet him by the road, but then I noticed my boss Elby's car, then another car, then another car, and another car! Elby had closed the translation office that afternoon so that the entire staff could come to my house in a caravan to say good-bye to me! It was an achingly beautiful, sad moment filled with hugs and tears that reminded me how precious friendship and kindness really are. Isn't it wonderful how life can sometimes pull on your heartstrings? I actually think the heart benefits from little tugs once in a while. Sweet moments like these give the heart more strength and help it recover from the big breaks.

It's not every day that you leave a hotel and head to JFK at 4:30 a.m. with a miniature schnauzer on a one-way trip out west. To add to the excitement, as I tried to board the hotel's airport shuttle bus, I realized that the huge crate that the airport had insisted I buy did not fit through the shuttle door. With the speed of a mechanic, I undid all eight screws latching the top of the crate to the bottom, disassembled the door, inverted the top, and placed it into the bottom of the crate, shoving all the nuts and bolts into my pocket. Needless to say, the other passengers staring at me through the shuttle windows were not impressed by the delay. *How was I to know the thing wouldn't fit through the door?* When we were finally seated, Bear sat quietly on my lap and leaned his little body as hard as he could into mine as if to say, "As long as I'm with you, Mommy, everything will be fine." Arriving at the airport, I gave Bear one last opportunity for a pee break, placed him in his reassembled crate, and watched the airport staff wheel him away. Like a mother sending her child off on the first day of school, I tried to be brave for his sake—though, in truth, I needed a Valium. When the crate finally rolled out of sight, my separation anxiety kicked in, and I considered letting out a whimpering howl. In the end, I decided it would be more humanlike if I distracted myself with rich pastries and copious amounts of Starbucks coffee.

It was a long flight, but I was comforted by the thought that Mom would be waiting for me with open arms at the Seattle airport. I knew she would arrive there much too early (as she always did), and I knew she would figure out just where to meet me. After landing and exchanging our big hugs, Mom and I rushed to the office where you retrieve animals. The airport staff explained that Bear would arrive shortly. I spotted a crate being wheeled through the large crowd of people, but no sound was coming from it. I thought, *Oh, goodness, is that Bear? Is he OK?* When the crate finally came into view and Bear heard my voice, he started screeching. It was not a bark or a howl but sounded more like a loud mob of seagulls fighting over a fish. His little paws were plastered against the crate door as he tried to get to me. I asked the airport porter, "Can I take him out?"

The man said, "Please do!"

As Bear leaped into my arms, he continued his screeching, wagged his stubby tail at a furious pace, and was obviously overcome with joy at seeing me. He then spotted my mother standing beside me and leaned toward her to give her a big, sloppy kiss all up her cheek. By then, everyone in the airport had stopped to look and laugh. The woman in charge of pet cargo walked up to me with a big grin on her face and said, "I don't think I have to ask for your ID!"

"Yes," I replied, "he's mine, all right!"

As Mom drove me to my new home, Bear slept coma-like in the backseat of her car, snoring with his mouth open like an old man. Yes, he and I could both relax now—we were together again. As we left the airport, I realized spring had already arrived in Washington State, and the cherry blossoms were in full, pink bloom. Just like my mother's open arms, nature too seemed to be offering a warm welcome.

During our first summer in Washington State, we experienced the best form of trickery. It was March of 2004, and that summer was one of the nicest, sunniest summers on record. We enjoyed day after day of fabulous weather. *What was all that talk about rain?* Imagine the sheer beauty of the Pacific Northwest combined with sunshine in the high seventies, low eighties—nothing could seem better. Everyone warned us that it was really, *really* not normal, but we enjoyed our honeymoon with the Evergreen State nevertheless.

Sadly, a honeymoon, like the moon itself, can take new forms and sometimes seems only a quarter of what it once was. When a deep, gray drizzle set in in late fall, I assumed the rain and overcast weather would end in a few days. *Of course*, I said to myself, *one week, tops*. When that week passed and the only variation in the sky was between dark gray and light gray, I said to myself, *Well, I guess it is possible it could be overcast for a month.* By February, I started fervently praying to God to send a strong wind to part the clouds like the Red Sea and bathe our town in strong sunshine. Unfortunately, my name must have been missing from God's good books that winter, for we had to wait until the following July before enjoying our first two weeks of fine, sunny weather. Of course, it doesn't drizzle constantly in all parts of Washington. In fact, there are some regions of the state that see the blessed sun—just not ours. No, we were tucked up in the far northwest corner where we quickly discovered that nature has a mean streak—for she often teased us with strong sunshine for a blissful afternoon and then cruelly followed that up with ten days of rain.

I must admit, though, that a nomadic life does have its advantages. First, one's understanding of geography improves. I now know that Washington State is left of Idaho and above Oregon. Washington is where Boeing is headquartered, where Bill Gates and Microsoft reside, and where Starbucks started pouring its deliciously addictive coffee. The state is green in all respects and produces the most tantalizingly sweet and crisp apples. Interestingly, Washington also has some of the largest tulip farms outside of Holland, and its moderate climate produces the happiest rhododendrons and azaleas I've ever seen. Many horse farms dot the landscape, and even at a distance, I could see the horses relishing their lush, tasty pastures. With all that grass to gobble and with the rain keeping the flies at bay, the horses in our town sure seemed a contented lot.

When I finally finished unpacking and put the always-dependable box cutter away, I started looking for a new riding instructor. I found a fourth-level dressage trainer in Lynden. Since she was fourth level and my previous instructor had only been third level, I assumed better things were to come.

My first lesson was memorable, to say the least. My new instructor, Annette, was what I call a hard-looking woman in her early fifties. Her arms and hands made her look strong as an ox, and it was clear she had spent many years out in the elements without giving a moment's thought to facial cream or sun block. Her eyebrows were au naturel, and her frizzy hair, which looked like it had undergone some sort of shock treatment, was unevenly cut. For some reason, I immediately imagined her chopping firewood at the bottom of a snowy mountain or driving an eighteen-wheeler truck. She looked like someone who could drink with the boys and handle herself in a brawl. My first impression of her personality: intense.

After introducing myself, I explained, "I've been riding off and on since I was nine years old. I'm an average rider, and I'd like to learn more about dressage."

"Well," she said in a very grave tone, "dressage is something that you cannot take lightly. It takes real commitment to succeed in dressage." She then told me about all the sacrifices she had made in her life to get to her level of expertise. At times, she would drive days and nights just to receive one lesson from an important dressage instructor. She told me how she had worked two jobs so that she could afford her horses—and these were, she assured me, *very* valuable horses. She described in great detail the many clinics she had attended and how she would question her instructors and how they would often agree with her views. At the end of this introductory speech and with the seriousness of a navy recruiter, she said, "It takes years to succeed in dressage. Have you asked yourself whether you are willing to make such a commitment?"

I knew my love of horses ran deep, but I didn't see myself driving day and night anywhere to take one lesson. In truth, I don't like driving more than an hour in any direction. Looking into her demanding eyes, however, I felt a strong need to salute and say, "Dressage is my life, sir!" Instead, I replied meekly, "I would like to learn more."

Annette looked at me a little suspiciously and proceeded to lead me to the barn. I say *lead* because she marched ten steps ahead of me, and I followed like an obedient sheepdog. As we approached the barn, she barked orders at a worker to not forget to turn on the electric wire of pasture number three. Entering the stable, I was pleased to see that my assigned school horse was a beautiful, bay Hanoverian. When I commented on his good looks, Annette looked at me with great pride and explained that he was twenty-seven years old. *Boy*, I thought, *she really doesn't trust me from the get-go. I mean, she is obviously putting me on the oldest horse she has.* She allowed me to groom the horse, but she didn't allow me to put the saddle or the bridle on. Until she knew my skill level, I was not to be trusted. She then demonstrated her own saddling and bridling technique, which (I was pleased to see) was identical to the way I had been saddling and bridling *forever*.

During the tacking-up process, she talked with another boarder, complaining how the farrier had not shown up, how the hay had had to be sent back because it was moldy, how the water troughs had overflowed, and how the dog had eaten too much manure and thrown up again. Stable management, apparently, has its issues. I stood quietly beside my mount, too intimidated to interject anything into the conversation.

Annette began my lesson before we even left the barn. She told me she was going to teach me how to lead a horse. I thought, *Holy crow, lady, I think I can walk beside a horse!*

"OK," she said, "show me how *you* lead a horse." With bated breath (actually, I don't think I breathed at all), I walked the horse up and down the driveway adjacent to the barn. Apparently, I wasn't bad at leading, but I was instructed to walk faster. "It is extremely important to walk quickly and not dawdle. The horse must feel you are the boss, and you must walk purposefully!" she explained. I then did my best speed walk, and the horse kept up without missing a beat. He had obviously been told about the fast-walking rule. When we eventually made it to the riding arena, I led my horse to the mounting block, expecting to get on. "Oh, no!" Annette cried out. "We *never ever* ride until we have longed a horse first.

Horses *must* be allowed to warm up before we put added weight on their backs."

It was a warm day, and the twenty-seven-year-old horse looked calm as a cucumber. At 125 pounds, I didn't think I was a weight to be contended with, *but whatever.* Annette then proceeded to demonstrate proper longing techniques. I had never longed a horse myself before, and I was actually excited about the idea of trying something new. Annette's demonstration lasted longer than I expected, and before I knew it, the lesson had ended.

When I got home that night, Kam muted the television and asked excitedly, "Hey, how did your ride go?"

"It went well, but I didn't ride. I learned how to longe a horse."

"Oh, so you longed the horse yourself?" Kam asked.

"No, not quite," I said. "I watched how the instructor longes and learned a lot in the process. She really knows a lot and is quite accomplished."

"So you didn't even get on the horse?" he asked in disbelief.

"No, but I get to ride next week."

LIFE WITHOUT STIRRUPS

"Oh, OK, that's good. As long as you had fun," he replied and went back to his show.

But I didn't get to ride the following week. For the next six weeks, I was only allowed to longe. Yes, I was in longeing boot camp, and only after passing this stage would I actually get to ride. I felt incredibly awkward at first. Like riding, longeing seems very easy until you try it. Longeing usually takes place in a round, fenced pen where the horse circles around the rider. The practice is used as an equine training tool, as a form of exercise for the horse, and as a way to let a horse blow off steam or warm up before you get on it. Horses that have been cooped up in a stall all day can have a lot of pent-up energy—especially young horses. So, unless you want to be catapulted through the air or enjoy the challenge of riding a bucking bronco, it is often a good idea to let a horse jump about with glee in a round pen before you set foot in a stirrup.

When longeing a horse in a large arena (as we were doing) rather than in an enclosed, round pen, you have to hold a longe line (a long rope that is attached to the horse's halter) in one hand and the whip in your other while the horse travels in circles around you. Continuously turning, you have to keep your body essentially parallel to the horse's body, getting neither too far behind nor too far in front of the horse's movement. While you do this spinning, you have to pay attention to the horse to see if it is relaxed and listening to your cues and gauge whether it is walking and trotting with the right momentum or cantering on the correct lead. On top of all this, you have to make sure the horse doesn't cut his corners, doesn't tug on the longe line, and doesn't circle around you with his nose pointed away from you.

While I longed, Annette would stand at the side of the arena, barking out orders. At first, I felt like I was in a spinning version of Simon Says. Initially, the only thoughts that filled my mind were, *Try not to faint, try not to faint. You're dizzy, but don't fall on your face in front of this woman.* Then it was, *Shoot, I've got the longe line all tangled up again. Don't let it get wrapped around your hand, or you'll be dragged around the arena!* Every so often, Annette would machine-gun questions at me, like, "Is the horse on the correct lead?" I would then try to focus my eyes through the spinning haze and decipher how the horse's front feet were landing. Sometimes I would forget to move my own feet, concentrating as I was on the horse's, and end up in a tight body twist with my head in an *Exorcist*-style position. To top everything off, Annette had developed a personal theory (and I say *personal* because I've never heard anyone else say this) that all successful horsemanship is related to the position of one's belly button. Yes, in order to longe and ride properly, you have to be very conscious of your belly button. As such, while I was circling and trying to concentrate on moving my feet and holding my hands correctly, I also had to push my belly button outward (in a *D* position) and thus bring my shoulders back. I don't know about the horse, but after an hour of one of Annette's longeing lessons, I was mentally and physically exhausted.

It was only weeks later, after I graduated from longeing boot camp, that I was finally allowed to get on the horse. By then, I was used to Annette's bellowing and unfazed by her directness. I thought, *Just ride the best you can. You know a lot more now. You won't make a fool of yourself. Remember, you had those dressage lessons in Connecticut.* To start off, Annette directed me to walk the horse clockwise around the arena and make a circle at the other end. The horse seemed calm enough, and we set off at an energetic walk, determined not to dawdle.

When I reached the end of the arena and asked the horse to turn right, the horse went left. I stopped, shocked. I yelled back to Annette, who was still at the far end of the arena, "There is something wrong with your horse! I asked him to turn right, and he went left!"

"No," she said, "you thought you asked him to turn right, but you actually told him to go left."

"*No*, I asked him to turn right, and he went left!" I replied with polite emphasis.

"Try it again," she ordered.

So we walked forward, and when I got to the corner, I pulled back slightly with my right rein (in other words, I used a direct rein), and the horse went *left* and walked straight into the wall of the arena.

"You see," she explained, "you have never ridden such well-trained horses before. These horses are trained to respond to the slightest shift in your body weight and the amount of contact you have with the reins. Your pelvis tilted the wrong way, and that is why the horse went left. This is the way you should have been taught all along, but you were taught incorrectly." *Oh, goodness gracious*, I thought. *All this time, I was doing it wrong! But whenever I asked a horse to go right before, it worked perfectly.* During that lesson, I was unable to get her horse to make one decent turn. This woman seemed so accomplished, and here, I couldn't even turn a horse left or right properly.

When I arrived home that night, Kam asked, "So, how was your lesson? Did you finally get to ride?"

"Ya, I rode today."

"So, how was it?"

"Terrible. I couldn't make the horse turn."

"What do you mean, you couldn't make the horse turn? I've seen you do a gazillion circles!"

"Apparently, her horses are really advanced, and the way I learned how to ask for a turn is all wrong," I replied, almost ready to cry.

"Don't worry, hon," said Kam as he took me in his arms. "You'll get the hang of it." Then, to make me laugh, Kam added, "At the next lesson, just ride straight. When she asks you to turn, ride straight out of the arena!"

Unfortunately, my inability to turn persisted. Annette, I, and the unlucky horse practiced and practiced. Annette would try to get me to turn at a walk. When that didn't work, we tried it at a trot. Trying to turn right at the trot was even more embarrassing, because the horse would veer left quickly, and we would almost bash into the wall. The horse did appear to be listening to whatever miscues I was giving him. It got to the point that I would tense up prior to each turn and on approach start praying: *Please turn right, please turn right, please... dammit!* Annette explained that my riding techniques were all wrong. Apparently, while seated on the horse, I would drop my pelvis to one side and collapse at the hip. I also did not keep my shoulders back enough, and my belly button was never in the correct *D* position. Under her guidance, I began to ride like a stiff soldier. I would push my stomach out and try to hold my shoulders back. She would then ask me to ride taller and imagine I was a puppet with a string coming out of my head and someone was pulling me skyward. I responded by adopting a stiff upper-body position and spent most lessons trying to concentrate on where my seat bones were.

After weeks of trying to master a simple turn with no success, I finally broke down at the end of a lesson and started to sob quite pathetically. Annette, temporarily softening her rough demeanor, tried to console me. She mentioned a riding clinic she was having that included a beach ride and that I should attend. It would be two full days of intense instruction, and she was sure I would get it then. "You'll see. At the clinic, everything will come together."

"Really?" I said, wiping away the tears. "OK, I'll come."

As I drove home from my lesson that night, it was clear I had hit rock bottom. *Maybe I should just quit. I can't even turn right. I'm the most pathetic rider ever. Why do you want to put yourself through this? A hobby is supposed to be fun! This is making you so crazy! And now look at you, a grown woman, crying like a baby because of a riding lesson! Why don't you quit and be done with it?* But somewhere deep inside was this little voice that said, "No, you can't quit." I don't know if it was stubbornness or stupidity, but I was going to ride on.

When clinic day did arrive, even though I was still a little depressed about my riding, I tried to muster up a positive attitude. There were eight women from all walks of life and riding experiences attending the clinic. Some of the participants had brought their own horses, while Annette trailered in her horses for the session. I borrowed my usual lesson horse. The clinic was a combination of lecture and riding instruction. It was interesting to see Annette in action. She was quite the little self-promoter, but I guess you do have to convince the participants it's worth their while to shell out $350 for a weekend of riding instruction. I actually rode a bit better during the clinic. I think it was because Annette's attention was often elsewhere and I could relax. I also realized that I needed a bit of quiet to actually think through what I was doing.

The advertised highlight of the clinic was the beach ride, so all the participants were excitedly looking forward to Sunday when it was to take place. On Sunday morning, our riding lessons wrapped up at 11:30 a.m., and after lunch, we all trailered our horses over to the magnificent Pacific Ocean. By the time we arrived, the morning fog had lifted, and the sun was peeking through the clouds. There was a fairly strong breeze that afternoon, and the smell of salt and sea filled the air. The beach was incredibly wide, and the powdery sand seemed to run endlessly for miles and miles. Because of the wind, the surf was rough, and white breakers were roaring in at regular intervals onto the sand. To my surprise, there were horse trailers everywhere, and people were riding horses along the beach in every direction.

As we drove the rigs onto some hard-packed sand, all I wanted to do was enjoy a good gallop with the wind in my hair. We pulled the trailers up to red markers, beyond which you weren't allowed to park, and then unloaded the horses. The horses were so excited and happy—you could just see it in their shiny eyes. They were looking at everything, pawing the sand exuberantly, and taking in big breaths to smell the sea. We clinic participants tacked up our horses and waited for Annette to mount up and lead us on our ride. Then it happened. Rather than getting on her horse, Annette started searching through a large, canvas bag, only to pull out dressage letters! *Oh God*, I thought. *NO. You wouldn't! You couldn't do that to us!*

For those of you who might not understand the implications of this, dressage letters are the letters you see at different points of a typical dressage arena. The letters help guide you, marking the points at which you change direction or change your speed. You ride from A to C or across the diagonal from H to F. Much to our horror, Annette proceeded to walk toward the ocean and carefully place all the dressage letters on the sand in their usual spots. Yes, she was going to make us ride in circles on this magnificent beach. At that point, I considered pretending lack of control and setting off at a mad, screaming gallop on my own. Sadly, we were all wimps and too meek to mutiny. So, there we were, riding in circles with the Pacific Ocean in the background. All I could hear in my head was the sound of my brother's mocking voice. *"Boy, you dressage riders sure know how to live it up!"* Even the other people on the beach enjoying a stroll or riding by us thought we were mad.

After our training, Annette did take us for a little ride up the beach, but there was *no cantering or galloping allowed*. "No, that is too dangerous for the horses," Annette said. "They might strain a ligament." The horses, however, would have just loved a good run, strained ligament or not. I began to think this woman had a screw loose! I probably would have parted ways with her that weekend, but a week prior, I had asked Annette to give Kam a lesson. With the lesson already scheduled, I didn't want to cancel it. I also wanted to see what Kam thought about her. I knew he would give me his honest opinion. Perhaps I was being too judgmental.

When the day finally came for his ride, I asked Annette not to go into longeing. "Kam, being a guy, just wants to know the basics," I said with emphasis. She said she understood and promised to let him ride. Even during his lesson, I could see Kam was quite amused by her belly-button theory. He then began to ride with his belly shoved forward and his shoulders arched back stiffly. As soon as he got in the car for the ride home he said, "That woman can't teach. I was so confused. I can't believe you wasted all that money taking lessons from her. Find someone else!"

"OK," I said with a sigh of relief. Decision made. I trusted Kam's judgment even better than my own.

It was odd how guilty I felt about the whole thing. Despite her quirks, I had come to like Annette as a person, and I felt I was betraying her by seeking instruction elsewhere. I had learned a lot from her in many ways—it was just that under her instruction, I felt I was stepping backward when I wanted to move forward—or at least turn right. And I finally had come to the conclusion that it didn't matter if I sucked at riding. Horses were in my blood, and I just couldn't wash them away. It was at that very moment, when my self-esteem was lying prostrate at the bottom of a wheelbarrow, that I finally let go of my ego and began to laugh at myself. As it turned out, this was just the cure I needed.

8

In Search of a Male Riding Instructor

Without warning, my husband decided to place a carrot at the end of a very long stick. "If you find a male riding instructor, I'll take lessons with you."

"Really?" I said with delight, for this seemed like genuine, uncoerced interest in horseback riding. "But why do you care whether the instructor is male or female?" I asked, perplexed.

"I don't want to be the only guy at the barn," Kam replied.

It was during his brief stint taking lessons in Quebec that Kam had first remarked, "Horses are a girl thing, aren't they?" There is certainly some truth to the observation. With the exception of cattle ranchers, jockeys, and those lightning-fast team ropers of the great state of Texas, I'd say the woman-to-man ratio at most barns ranges from seventy-thirty to ninety-ten. Learning to ride is usually something you are introduced to as a child or teenager, and I'm just not sure why young boys are less inclined to jump into the stirrups than girls.

It could be that boys, being protective of their little willies, find the idea of bouncing around in a saddle a tad worrisome. Or perhaps, just as tight leotards can frighten boys away from dance classes, the idea of pulling up a pair of riding breeches strikes fear into their hearts? Of course, all that horse brushing does look a little girly. Women, on the other hand, have no qualms about riding attire and will usually jump at the opportunity to brush a tangled mane to perfection. Furthermore, at least for some females, the idea of galloping away on a stallion is just much more exciting than being rescued by Prince Charming.

My personal theory is that women relate better to equine sensitivities. Certainly, there are some important parallels between women and horses. Horses, although imposing in size and quite capable of doing a lot of damage when they put their minds to it, will often run in complete panic from horribly scary objects such as an innocent plastic grocery bag floating gently across the ground. Women, too, can be subject to irrational responses. I myself am inclined to jump screaming onto beds, tables, or anything elevated at the mere sight of a tiny and equally innocent mouse scurrying across the bedroom floor. Whatever the real reason, many of us fillies have jumped headstrong into equine affairs.

Of course, it wasn't always this way. I'm sure some women in history had to fight their way into the saddle. I sometimes wonder who the first woman was to pick up the reins. Was it a Native American girl helping with the buffalo hunt, or a European woman trying to ride discreetly with her skirt to one side? I can only imagine the laughter of men enjoying a pint at the local tavern. "You women can ride, if you ride sidesaddle!" I guess we showed them! And who was the first grande dame to finally throw down her skirt, pull on a pair of trousers, and straddle on? Nowadays, women can ride as fast, jump as high, and fall as spectacularly as men can. In fact, equestrian events are one of the few Olympic sports where girls compete horse to horse with the boys.

Given equestrian demographics, I wasn't sure how difficult it was going to be to find a male riding instructor, but I sure wasn't going to lose the opportunity to rope Kam into the horse arena again, so I started calling local barns. "Yes, hello. I'm looking for a riding instructor for my husband, and he would prefer a male instructor. Do you know of any?

"Hmmm...no, can't say I do. Never met one."

"Yes, hello. I'm looking for a riding instructor for my husband, and he would prefer a male instructor. Do you know of any?

"A few years back, there was a guy who gave lessons just south of Bellingham, but there was a terrible accident. He was giving a trailer-loading demonstration to a large group of riders, and the horse he was working with started freaking out in the trailer. When the instructor tried to get the horse back out, it kicked him dead center, right in the heart. Poor guy died instantly. I must say, though, that the barn was good about it. They gave the students their money back."

"Oh, dear, so sorry to hear that. Thanks, anyway," I replied in a bit of shock. After hanging up the phone, I thought, *Well! I really didn't need to hear that!* And just as I push to the back of my mind the thought of dying in an airplane crash as I walk down the aisle of a 747, I buried the thought of being kicked in the heart by a horse to some deep, dark corner of my psyche.

"Yes, hello. I'm looking for a riding instructor for my husband, and he would prefer a male instructor. Do you know of any?

"What's wrong with a female instructor?" the woman replied with indignation.

"No, nothing's wrong with a woman. It's just that my husband would probably feel more at ease with a male instructor. It's a guy thing. Do you know of anyone?"

"The only person I know around here is Tom, and he's at Peace Arch."

"Do you mean the Peace Arch that straddles the US-Canadian border? Is his barn near the Arch itself?" I replied, dumbfounded, for the Peace Arch was a gigantic, white arch that straddled the international border between Washington State and British Columbia.

"No; the name of his place is the Peace Arch Equestrian Center."

"Oh, OK. Thanks."

After finally finding the number in the phone book, I called. "Yes, hello. I'm looking for Tom."

"This is he," replied a man suspiciously.

"And you're a horseback riding instructor?" I asked.

"Some people think so," he replied with a chuckle.

I thought I'd test Tom out before scheduling a lesson for Kam, so I signed myself up for a one-hour private. As it turned out, the equestrian center was a mere ten minutes from our house at the end of a lovely, densely treed, country road. The barn was quite large, with a metal-sided exterior and a green roof. Some metal pipe pens had been erected on the right side of the building, and I could see there was an outdoor riding ring just beyond them. Across the street was a good-sized, perhaps five-acre, parcel of land that had been electric fenced. About ten horses were in this large pasture, milling about peacefully, their noses shoved dutifully in the long grass as they mowed it down.

After parking on the gravel driveway, to enter the building, I pulled the heavy barn door to one side and was greeted by a very friendly and awfully scruffy black-and-white border collie whose fur was covered in sawdust. The dog had obviously just wakened from a nap, for it paused for a deep, doggy stretch before trotting submissively over to me. Petting the dog's soft head, I leaned over to pull a few strands of hay that had become tangled in its tail. The dog had a pink collar on, so holding its cheeks in the palm of my hands, I looked into its gentle eyes and said, "Are you a sweet girl?" The dog replied with a happy wag of its tail and led me through the barn as if she was my assigned tour guide.

The stable was designed like the letter H, with two parallel barn aisles joined together by a short corridor. The barn had one tack room in each aisle, and both were packed to the ceiling with all the normal tools of the trade—saddles, bridles, blankets, and grooming tools. As if to equitably divide the barn real estate and foster dog-feline peace, I noticed a well-worn dog bed in one tack room and a small cat bed and elevated cat-food bowls in the other. A covered riding arena was attached directly to the building. The arena was three sided and opened on the far side to a small forest of pine trees. Having only ridden in colder climates, I had never seen a covered riding arena that opened directly to the outdoors.

Taking a moment to look at the arena, I thought, *Yes, I guess it does make sense...in Washington State, one only needs protection from the rain and some way to keep the arena footing dry. With the constant drizzle, I can see the need to prevent a major mudfest where horses might slip and slide and end up splaying their long legs in awkward directions.* As I continued walking through the facility, I could see that the barn had seen better days. I kept a close eye on the metal roof, which looked precarious in spots and made me a tad nervous. I also noticed the fronts of the wooden stalls had deep gouges in them where some very bored horses must have chewed away for hours on end. Despite the obvious infrastructure challenges, the horses themselves seemed quite content and looked healthy, and their bedding was fresh and clean, which is always a good sign when one is scoping out a new barn.

As it turns out, the barn had had an interesting history. The original owner thought he could make good money boarding horses. When reality set in that horse boarding, in and of itself, is not a great moneymaking business, the owner tried "self-boarding." Essentially, he allowed people to stable their horses at the barn for a reduced rate, but they had to feed, muck stalls, and do all the work themselves. Human nature being what it is, this communal work share didn't work, and over time, the barn became a tired mess of unkempt stalls and mud-filled pens. When Tom approached the owner years later and offered to rent the whole place, the owner was only too delighted to have him. Tom cleaned the facility up as best he could, filled the barn with proper boarders and lesson horses, and started a riding-instruction program.

My introduction to that rare commodity—a male riding instructor—was a bit of a surprise. Walking down the far end of the barn aisle, I came across a farrier bent over and holding a horse's hoof between his knees. "Hi, I'm looking for Tom. Can you tell me where he is?"

"What do you want him for?" he asked without looking up at me.

"I have a riding lesson at two o'clock."

"Just hold on a sec," he said as he carefully examined the hoof angles, not letting my presence rush him a bit. When the man finally stood and wiped what few strands of hair he had left to one side of his head, he smiled and said, "Geez, you're early." It was only 1:00 p.m.

"The barn was closer to my house than I expected," I explained shyly, not wanting to confess that I was neurotic and would always arrive much too early. "Sorry, are you Tom? I thought you were the farrier," I asked, embarrassed.

"Yes, I'm Tom. I'm the riding instructor, the farrier, and the horse trainer, but not on Sundays," he replied matter-of-factly.

Tom was an older man (perhaps in his late fifties or early sixties) who looked like he belonged more in a John Wayne movie than in a small town in the Pacific Northwest. He was wearing faded blue jeans that he had paired with an equally faded and wrinkled blue-jean shirt. He sported tan leather cowboy boots that were deeply creased from age and brought his toes to a sharp point. As if to complete the image, as soon as he finished his farrier work, he quickly covered his receding hairline with a large, black cowboy hat. I later realized that this outfit never varied and was as dependable as he was.

Tom had been riding and training horses for over forty years. Although he didn't say a word to me about his credentials, I found out from other boarders later on that Tom was a Resistance Free® certified horse trainer and riding instructor, a certified farrier, and a certified equine myofunctional therapist (yes, horses get massages too). I guess he should have been wearing a T-shirt that said, "Been there, done that—over and over."

My first impression of Tom was that he was a gentle soul, quiet and a bit shy. After he put the newly shod horse back into one of the pastures, he calmly took the horse I was to ride out of its stall and led it to the indoor arena. He then tied the horse with a slipknot to a heavy post against the arena wall and returned to the barn to get the tack, setting it on the edge of a two-by-four. With the horse tied and ready, Tom then stopped and turned toward me. Keeping his eyes to the ground, as if intent on really listening to what I had to say, he then asked the fateful question: "So, tell me about your riding experience."

Looking at Tom with his head bowed like a priest ready to hear confession, I decided to tell the truth, the whole truth, and nothing but the truth, so help me God. "I've been riding off and on since I was nine years old, and I really suck at it." To convince him I wasn't joking, I added, "I've been taking dressage lessons for about two years in total, but I'm not a very good rider *at all*, not even on a good day...but I'm crazy about horses, and I just can't give riding up. I don't know why."

"So I guess you're not trying to get to the Olympics, then!" he joked.

"Yes, the Olympics are certainly out of the question."

To my surprise, he let me groom and tack up on my own. Tom just stood to one side, quietly observing me. I then asked where the longe whip was. "Why do you want a longe whip?" he asked, puzzled.

"Aren't we supposed to longe the horse first to make sure his back is warm?"

He kind of chuckled and said, "Well, it's not that cold out! Oh, of course, we do longe horses, especially the young ones, to train them. And if a horse has been in a stall all day, you might want to longe him to let him let off some steam, but this horse has been in the pasture today, and he doesn't need to be longed."

"Oh, I thought I had to longe every time before I rode."

"Well, that would get awfully tiring now, wouldn't it? Seems like a lot of work to me. Don't you want to just get on a horse and ride down a trail sometimes?" I had to smile. Boy, that sounded nice. I decided not to tell Tom in advance about my horse-turning issues. I just wanted to see what happened when I rode and tried to turn.

My lesson horse was a paint with bold patches of black on white. He was aptly named Domino and reminded me of the ace of spades. I asked how old the horse was, and I was told he was only four years old. *Goodness gracious,* I thought—*putting me on a four-year-old when he hasn't seen me ride!* Tom assured me the horse had a lot of experience, was very calm, and that he had trained him himself.

After mounting, I gathered up the reins and headed off down the side of the arena at a walk. Tom's only instruction was, "Just do whatever you like. I'm just going to sit here and watch you ride. I want to get a better sense of what you know and don't know."

I rode parallel to the arena wall, and when I got to the corner, I pulled back ever so slightly on the right rein. The horse calmly turned right. It was a miracle! After circling once to the right, I decided to change direction and asked the horse with a light nudge on the left rein to turn left. The horse turned left. I then stopped and, grinning from ear to ear, looked at Tom and said, "I turned the horse! He turned right and left!"

Tom, at this point, thought I was a bit mad. "Didn't you tell me you'd been riding off and on since you were nine years old and took dressage lessons?"

"Yes," I stammered. "But at the previous barn, I was riding these really highly trained advanced dressage horses but couldn't get them to turn right or left. It was just so hard."

"Hmmm," He said. "Interesting...doesn't sound like they were well trained to me."

I then with pure and utter delight spent the rest of the lesson doing circles and figure eights, feeling as happy as if I had won the lottery. This horse seemed to understand what I wanted and did what I asked. Although I was a little nervous,

I walked, trotted, and even cantered the horse in both directions, throwing in joyous circles whenever I could. It was strange deciding all by myself which way to turn or what speed to ride at. For so many years, I had always waited for an instructor to tell me whether I was to ride clockwise or counterclockwise or when and where I was to transition from trot to canter or canter to trot. I almost felt like a dog whose owner had finally let him off leash and stopped pulling him in specific directions. And, like a dog off leash erratically running left and then right, in my excitement, I think I put that horse through every pace, curve, diagonal, and transition I had ever learned.

When my hour was nearly up, Tom finally asked a few questions. "Did the horse do what you wanted him to do?"

"Yes."

"Did you have to use force or strong aids to get the horse to do what you wanted?"

"No."

"Was the horse calm and relaxed?"

"Yes."

"Then you did it correctly. That's how you tell if you're doing things right."

"What do you mean?" I said.

"What's the most important thing when riding? What do you want to aim for?" he asked.

I wasn't sure what to answer and suspected it was a trick question, so I shrugged my shoulders. "Calmness and relaxation," Tom said. "If a horse does what you want it to do, when you want to do it, and stays calm and relaxed, you know you are doing things right." Tom didn't say much else. He ended the lesson with a simple, "After you untack, make sure you cool the horse out first before you put him back in the stall." He started walking away down the barn aisle and then paused and looked back at me. "Oh, and by the way, you're not as bad as you think you are." And with that, he left.

For the first time in a very long time, I felt good about my riding. I felt happy. Also, to my surprise, I felt a great deal of "calmness and relaxation."

9

Time Was Ticking

I first realized the value of different teaching methods when I was seven years old. My father, quite out of the blue, decided that he was going to teach his darling daughter how to tell the time. I don't know what inspired him to take on this task—perhaps I had been showing up late for dinner? Or maybe I wasn't standing sufficiently long in corners during punishment? For whatever reason and with unusual seriousness, one Sunday evening, Dad sat me down at the kitchen table and began explaining to me that there were sixty seconds in a minute, sixty minutes in an hour, twelve hours in a day, twelve hours in a night, twenty-four hours in a day, and 365 days in a year.

In his lecture, he went on to explain how time relates to how fast the earth rotates around the sun and how the world is made up of different time zones. To round out his rather formal presentation, he pulled a blank piece of paper out of a kitchen drawer and made diagrams of the earth rotating around the sun. Pleased as punch with this one-on-one attention, I smiled encouragingly at him throughout the lecture. Suddenly, as if inspired to make my learning experience as interesting as possible, he jumped up on a chair and carefully took the kitchen clock down from the wall, setting it in the middle of the table. Until then, I hadn't noticed the clock, but now that it was set dead center on the table, it looked rather ominous—more like a bomb about to explode.

Dad then delved into the concepts of clockwise and counterclockwise, twisting the arms of the clock in both directions. Then, and without the slightest warning, he adjusted the arms of the clock, turned the clock face toward me, and asked me what time it was. I had no idea, as the only part of his teaching I remembered was that the earth goes around the sun. Seeing my blank stare, he returned to the sixty-minutes-in-an-hour concept and then asked me again, "Dagny, what time is it?"

With a big grin and considerable enthusiasm, I answered, "One hundred!" Seemed like a good choice at the time—after all, it was the number I was told to aim for in school.

"No. Try again," Dad said, placing the clock hands in different positions and holding the clock face closer to me, as if perhaps it was my eyesight that was the problem. After several wrong answers on my part, Dad, his forehead creased in genuine concern, slowly got up from the table and left me to go downstairs to the TV room. "We'll continue our studies another day," he said with a sigh as he descended to the basement.

I was staring at the terrible clock when my mother came into the room. "What's wrong, Dagny"?

"Daddy tried to teach me how to tell time, and I don't understand!" I was upset and began to cry.

"OK," she said as she sat down beside me at the table, pulled me onto her lap, and said, "Show me how you can count by fives." We had just learned that in school, so I rolled off the count. "Five, ten, fifteen, twenty..." all the way to one hundred.

"Great," said Mom as she picked up the clock in her hands, turning it toward me. "When you look at a clock, first say the number that the little hand is pointed to." She then moved the little hand to the two. "OK. Say the number."

I said "Two," wiping away my tears.

"After you say the number that the little hand points to, you look at where the big hand is and count to it like this:

'five, ten, fifteen, twenty...'" She then rolled the little hand to the number three and pointed to it. "What time is it?"

"Three," I answered with more confidence.

Turning the little hand to four and the big hand to three, she asked, "What time is it now?"

I paused and then meekly said, "Four fifteen?"

"Yes!" she said with a big smile. Then she moved the big hand to the nine. "Now this one is harder. What is it now? And remember to count."

I had to concentrate, but then I said, "Four forty-five?"

"Bravo! You did it!"

Elated, I ran down the stairs to proudly demonstrate my clock-reading skills to my father. "Daddy! Mommy taught me how to tell the time!"

It had taken my mother five minutes to teach me how to read a clock. Of course, later on, the concepts of sixty seconds in a minute and sixty minutes in an hour did gel in my young brain, and I saw the merits of my father's explanations. Dad wanted to explain time from its fundamental, root concepts, whereas my mother gave me a pragmatic trick to read the clock. Her method was effective and provided results, but understanding the fundamentals is important too.

Of course, even as an adult, I have a mere mortal's understanding of time and am no Steven Hawking. For example, I do understand how precious time is and that it is important to always be on time and never waste time. And I do see how time is slowly adding crow's feet to my eyes and robbing color from my hair. Given that time seems the universe's most abundant gift, I've always thought we humans must be a terribly greedy lot, as we never seem to get enough of it. As time passes, I have come to appreciate how dependable it is—ticking forward as it does without the slightest pause as the earth whirls around the sun, for millennia. Of course, if the earth stops all its circling and decides to go straight one day like a horse finally escaping the riding ring, I'll be back to where I started and won't know what time it is.

After I started taking horseback riding lessons with Tom, I realized that while I had learned a few riding tricks over the years, I really did not understand the fundamentals and had missed some core concepts. One of the most important concepts that I had failed to grasp was that horses are taught to move away from pressure and that the release of pressure is their reward. Certainly, I had squeezed my legs and made a horse move forward, but I had never understood that the release of the pressure of my legs and the timing with which I released it was extremely important. And while I had pulled back on the reins to make a horse stop, I learned that the timing and speed with which I released the pressure is pretty significant to the horse. Indeed, releasing pressure is like saying, "Yes, well done!" or "Thank you so much!" to a horse. "Always remember," Tom would say, "release is the reward."

Tom's teaching style was different from that of any of my other riding instructors. Thankfully, he was always punctual for his lessons, and when you were riding, you had 100 percent of his attention. He had a knack for remembering what we had worked on in the previous lesson, and in every new lesson, we would work on improving just one thing. I guess he knew not to overwhelm me by trying to fix too many of my bad habits at once. Rather than stand in the center of the arena as all my other instructors had done, Tom preferred to sit at the far end of it on a large, rusted metal barrel he had turned on its side and wedged perfectly into one corner. Tom, not being a tall man, would take a little jump to get up onto the barrel, then once on board, he'd sit there, casually swaying his pointy boots to and fro like a cowboy waiting for a parade to start.

Only when the horse and I approached his corner would he quietly give me instructions as I rode by. Sometimes he would ask me a question to test my knowledge or to try to figure out if I had really grasped what he had said. When I did get tense, he'd motion me to his corner, where I'd stop the horse and he'd take a moment to tell a joke or distract me with a funny horse story. For him, people were always in too much of a rush—too much of a rush to succeed at riding and too much of a rush when training a horse. He explained, "People just want results immediately, and if they don't get the results they want with the horse they are riding, they blame the horse and get another one. In fact, most horse problems are people problems."

Tom was the epitome of patience, and he had a way of inspiring people to have more of it too—more patience with their horses and more patience with themselves. I also appreciated the fact that even though he rode Western style, Tom didn't believe in spurs or harsh bits. But he did believe in riding helmets. In fact, when new students asked if they had to wear riding helmets, he'd often say, "Helmets are required only if you care about your ability to think." He led by example and always wore a helmet when he rode.

In fact, Tom had a stock story he used to convince people how important helmets are. As the story goes, one day, he was leading a group of students on a ride through a thickly forested trail near the barn. He was in the lead and had just turned a corner around some trees when he and his horse came face-to-face with a giant bald eagle perched on the ground over a kill. I would have thought this part of the story a bit farfetched, but since moving to Washington State, I had noticed that bald eagles are common to the area. Indeed, I often saw them perched at the very tops of trees, their dramatic black wings and white heads standing out magnificently against the gray skies. Well, as Tom explained, as soon as that eagle saw him, it lifted its six-foot wingspan into the air to fly away. Equally startled, Tom's horse decided to fly in the opposite direction, spinning 180 degrees in less than a second and whipping Tom into the trunk of a tree as it took off at a gallop. "I was mighty glad I had my helmet on that day," Tom said. "It doesn't matter how good a rider you are. Riding can be dangerous, and a helmet can save your life!"

"Wow!" I laughed. "Your students must have been impressed to see their instructor hit dirt!"

"Yeah," Tom replied with a chuckle, "it was a bit embarrassing, but luckily, by the time they reached that same corner with their horses, the bird was gone."

"What happened to your horse?"

"The darn thing was so frightened, it ran clear back to the barn and right into its stall!" Tom laughed.

Once I realized I had a gem of a resource in Tom, I decided to chisel away at his horse-savvy brain. I would arrive each week for my lesson with a specific, preplanned question. One week, it would be, "So, what is laminitis?" The next week was, "So, Tom, how do you tell if a horse colics?" or "What does it mean when a horse 'gets cast,' and how do I fix it?" Tom just seemed to know the answers, and no matter how hard I tried, I couldn't stump him. He always explained things in pragmatic, matter-of-fact ways, although some of his solutions did seem harder than others.

For example, a horse "getting cast" means the dumb horse lies down, gets its feet stuck against the wall of its stall, and can't get up. This can happen if the horse lies down too close to the wall and doesn't have enough space to get its legs under it or if the horse somehow lies down and then gets its legs caught between fence rails. Tom's solution to deal with a horse cast in a stall was to loop a long rope around the horse's front legs and another around its back legs and then pull the horse over on its back to the other side. As he was giving me this explanation, I remember making a mental note to either leave the fool horse be or call someone for help! No, I wasn't going to be roping a horse's legs like it was some cow. This was definitely a man's job, in my view. Yes, sometimes I'm just willing to forget all that women's lib and cry for help! But knowing Tom, he would have had the horse unstuck in a matter of moments and done it as calmly as if he was throwing a bale of hay.

In fact, sometimes Tom seemed too calm. I remember during one of my lessons, a boarder came running to the edge of the arena, completely panicked about a wound her horse had. Tom looked at her and said, "Is blood gushing out of him?"

"No," she replied, shaking her head.

"Aw, then he'll be fine. I'll check on him after the lesson."

It's not that Tom didn't care; it was just that he didn't panic. As a matter of fact, I remember one quiet, summer evening just as the sun was going down when I went to the barn to pick up a jacket I had forgotten and found Tom all alone, hand-walking one of the oldest school horses. He explained that the old mare had colicked, and although he had given her a painkiller, the horse still wasn't comfortable.

Since you may not know this little tidbit of equine anatomy, I should explain that horses are unable to throw up like we humans can. In fact, in my experience, the only thing they seem to be able to propel out of their mouths is any medicine you try to shove into them. While just the thought of throwing up or spending time heaving over a toilet makes me cringe, I now appreciate that this age-old human technique is actually a good thing for us mortals. I mean, sometimes one's stomach just can't take that much alcohol.

Horses, however, can have more serious "morning afters" than we do. When a horse colics, this means the animal is experiencing serious abdominal pain that can cause twisting of its intestines. Horses can colic simply because they don't drink enough water. Without water, food can get impacted in their stomachs and cause their intestines to distend. Horses can also colic when there is a buildup of gas in their digestive tracts or because they ingest too much sand from the ground as they eat. Stress can also cause a horse to colic. For example, horses often get stressed when we humans haul them long distances in horse trailers (especially if they aren't used to the process). Even quick changes in a horse's diet can cause a colic—and you thought horse grain was always well sealed just to prevent the mice from getting in it! Yes, many a wily horse and especially ponies are serious gluttons with the ability to plan sneak attacks on grain bins and give themselves colic in the process.

In fact, I once worked at a barn where the owners had to put a padlock on the feed room to keep one very crafty pony out of the grain. The pony feigned innocence and pretended not even to know where the grain was stored, always returning dutifully to its stall and shutting the door behind him before morning. But then there was that one night when things got out of hand. Yes, in hindsight, the pony had to admit it was a mistake to eat that second bag of grain. For, the next morning, the humans couldn't help but notice he was lying on his back, rolling from side to side. Of course, the fact that he had also gone cross-eyed was a dead giveaway. Luckily, the pony survived and, apart from having to endure a few snickers from his stable mates, was no worse for wear. No matter the reason—whether because of horse or human folly—when a horse does colic, vets will often tell you to keep the horse moving so that the horse passes gas and hopefully poops, as this can relieve pressure. Usually, one good poop is a sign that the horse is out of danger. So, unlike a human who can take a bow to the porcelain queen or reach for a Tums, horses have to walk it off.

I knew colic was a serious condition and that horses can even die from it, so I asked Tom, "How long have you been walking the mare for?"

"For about an hour."

"How long will you walk her?"

"For as long as it takes until she starts feeling better," he replied with determination in his voice.

After retrieving my jacket from the barn and knowing there was not much I could do to help, I got back into my car and sat for a moment, watching Tom lead that horse up and down the long, gravel driveway. It was an oddly beautiful moment. Tom, his black hat angled forward on his head as he stared at the ground in front of him, was leading the old mare in a sort of quiet, walking meditation. The last of the sun's rays were casting a warm glow over the horse's reddish coat while a few mourning doves perched on a telephone wire high above let out occasional, gentle coos. The barn's border collie was lying dutifully by the side of the barn. Resting her nose on the ground, she was using only her eyes to watch her master walk to and fro. Only the rhythmic sound of the horse's hooves crunching the gravel brought reality to the scene. Returning to the barn the next day, I looked for the old mare and found her in her stall, happily eating the last strands of morning hay. Noticing me, she stopped chewing momentarily and turned to look into my eyes as if to say, "No, it wasn't my time."

Although Kam's career didn't leave him much time for riding, he too was benefiting from Tom's instruction, taking regular weekly lessons and making horsey strides. I remember after his very first session with Tom, Kam said with enthusiasm, "Now, this guy can teach! And, you know, horses *are* really special creatures! Every time I'm with them, I just forget about work and any stress, and I just focus on what I'm doing—I'm just in the moment with them." I smiled and remembered the old saying, "The outside of a horse is good for the inside of a man." To me, it seemed ironic that the move to Washington State—a move I had dreaded to some extent—had ended up opening barn doors, bringing horses trotting into *both* of our lives, finally leading us to a good teacher who could help us through the paces.

As committed as ever to improving my understanding of all things horse, I signed up for every weekend riding clinic Tom offered. Poor Tom—it was almost comical to watch this quiet, soft-spoken man try to get groups of mostly chatty, middle-aged women to pay attention to him. I remember at one clinic, after waiting patiently for us to quiet down, Tom started his lecture with, "*Geez*, you women like to talk! You know, you women need to understand one thing," and then he paused. You could hear a pin drop. All I could think of was, *Tom, you better not say anything sexist to this crowd!* But then he smiled and said, "Horses are not dogs! They do not love you like a dog loves you. They just want to eat and be safe. When a horse comes running up to you in a pasture, it is not because he loves you. It is because he knows you are going to give him his grain."

"Awww," we replied in unison, "but we want our horses to love us!"

"I know," Tom said with a grin. "All you women are the same. You want the horse to love you, but it is more important that the horse respects you as its leader. There can only be one leader, and it's either you or him."

Darn it! I thought. I kind of liked the unconditional love idea.

As Tom explained, horses are herd animals, and when turned out together in a pasture, they will quickly establish hierarchy within the group. For example, if you have a group of five horses in a pasture, one will fight its way to the top and become boss horse, and then there will be a second-in-command, third-in-command, and so on. The weakest horse will be last on the totem pole. The boss horse will not necessarily be the oldest in the group; neither will it necessarily be a gelding. In fact, if you turn a mare out with a group of geldings, very often, the mare will end up as the boss. You see, mares often have the strength of character and willingness to kick a gelding's head off if he doesn't back off and concede to her superiority!

If you spend a little time watching a group of horses, it is often easy to figure out which horse is boss. You see, the boss horse gets to eat and drink first and hogs the best hay, not allowing others to take any of its feed. Also, whenever the boss horse walks directly into a group of horses, the others will part like the Red Sea and let it through. To give you a point of comparison, humans line up at a water fountain and wait patiently for a turn to drink, but in the horse world, the boss horse walks directly to the water trough, and the other horses had better get out of the way. You can think of the boss horse as the Al Capone of the herd.

One also has to realize that although horses do neigh and whinny, they are relatively silent creatures and mainly communicate with each other using body position and stance. Essentially, they establish their authority over other horses by making them move out of their space. As Tom explained to the clinic participants, "If you can get a horse to respect your personal space, the horse will think of you as boss horse. So it's really important to never let a horse walk into you or become pushy. A horse should always respect your space. People don't realize this, but if a horse steps toward you and you back up, you've just told that horse it's in charge." Tom then taught us some really easy techniques, like disengaging a horse's hip (which means circling a horse while making it move its hind end away from you) or making a horse back up eight or ten paces to establish your authority over it.

All of Tom's techniques were effective yet never involved hurting the horse. Yes, horse training has evolved over the years for the better. Many old cowboy techniques that involved a good deal of animal cruelty or attempts to break a horse's spirit are thankfully just not done anymore. And, just like parenting a naughty child, with a horse, you have to be firm and consistent and reward only good behavior. As Tom explained, "If every time a horse gets pushy with you, you make it back up ten paces, then the horse is going to think, 'Hey, I don't like all this backing up, and whenever I get pushy, this human makes me back up, so I guess I better stop being pushy.' It's as simple as that. You have to be consistent." Both Kam and I learned a great deal from Tom and for the first time started feeling like we were becoming real horse people.

Eventually, as my confidence as a rider improved, tiny little dream thoughts of horse ownership began percolating in my brain. In hindsight, those intervening years of not riding seemed like just an unfortunate blip in my life. In fact, any week of not riding now felt like having the flu—without my regular dose of equine, I was just out of sorts, sank into a general malaise, and, according to Kam, became prone to whining and crankiness. Furthermore, like a thirtyish woman who starts hearing the faint yet demanding tick of her biological clock, as I approached forty, I began hearing my horse-ownership clock. The tick started in the cerebral cortex, quickly morphed into a chime in the frontal lobe, and then settled into a demanding ring between my ears.

This was when my mind began staging regular arguments with me: *Why wait? Do you want to be fifty when you get your first horse?*

Now is the time. Go for it! You only live once! Yes, a horse can kill you, and yes, you don't want to become a paraplegic, but what are the odds of that happening? Don't be such a chicken! You will be just fine! Think positive! Yes, horses are really expensive, but it's just like having an additional car payment. And you have a kind, indulgent husband willing to hoof the bills. Come on! It's now or never! After turning the horse question over and over in my neurotic mind, I decided to toss a coin. It landed on tails, and I took that as a good sign. I mean, a horse does have a tail. *Yes, I would finally throw a bit of caution to the wind and buy my dream horse!* Little did I know that a dream sometimes comes with a shadow.

10

Buying the Evil Demon

Sometimes advice is sought but not followed.

For 3:00 p.m. on a Tuesday, the Aldergrove border crossing between the United States and Canada seemed unusually busy. Big, eighteen-wheeler trucks encircled the smallish customs building, filling the air with the smell of diesel fuel and the squeal of truck brakes. After finding a parking spot among these giants, I escaped into the customs office, where the roar of the trucks was slightly muted by the building's windows. The building itself was much like a fishbowl, with windows on three sides, giving the officers a clear view of oncoming vehicle lanes. Like all such places, the interior seemed strategically designed to make one feel uncomfortable. Hard, wooden chairs lined the pictureless, gray walls while imposing cameras were aimed down on those seated, tracking their every move.

As I approached the tall and very wide counter separating the customs officers from the people who needed questioning, I appreciated how lucky I was to be able to cross the US-Canada border without difficulty. As a Canadian living in the United States and a holder of the much-cherished green card, border crossings were a nonissue for me. This was obviously not the case for the mostly Mexican and Sikh truck drivers who were sitting anxiously on those uncomfortable chairs along the back wall.

"Can I help you, miss?" asked the customs officer.

"Oh, thanks," I replied. "I'm just waiting for a horse."

"How long have you been waiting?" asked the officer.

I paused, taking a moment for an inner smile, and then answered with a big grin, "My whole life!" But then I explained with a giggle, "No, I've only just arrived. The sellers are bringing my new horse over in their trailer, and he should be here soon. Where are the vet inspections done?"

"They're back there on the left side of the building," he replied, pointing me in the right direction.

Life is so unpredictable. Who would have thought that my childhood dream would begin at a small-town border crossing on a rainy day in Washington State? A few years earlier, I hadn't even known where Washington State was, yet here I was, waiting for my dream horse to arrive!

Trying to make conversation, the officer said, "I've owned a few horses in my day. What type of horse did you buy?"

"He's a three-year-old Arabian, my first horse."

"Well, you sure wanted a challenge, didn't you? I had an Arabian once," he said with a "never again" tone in his voice. "That horse was so crazy. He took off with me one day and almost killed us both. It didn't matter what I did; that horse never did settle down. I finally sold him and got myself a quiet paint quarter horse."

Just at that moment, I spotted a horse trailer approaching the building and excused myself, telling the officer that I had to go, my horse had arrived. Truthfully, I was glad to get away. I was already nervous enough about my new purchase, and I really didn't want to hear any more "Arabians are crazy" horse stories.

Initially, I hadn't really been set on buying an Arabian. I was seduced into it. You see, I found my horse the modern way—by searching Dreamhorse.com. Like a person using a dating website, I started out open-minded. My initial search was limited to the very neutral "horses for sale within a fifty-mile radius of my home" criterion. But just as women are attracted to good-looking men, only Arabians seemed to catch my eye. The beauty of the Arabian horse is legendary, and many consider the Arabian the most handsome of all. As a breed, Arabians are the long-distance athletes of the horse world. Like marathon runners, they have great stamina and endurance.

After much Googling, I discovered that Arabians are known for their intelligence; loyalty to their owners; good, hard feet; and great lung capacity. They also have a unique ability to disperse heat, and this helps them handle the rigors of traveling long distances and in hot weather. I also liked the fact that Arabians are generally smaller than other horses, and given I'm only five foot two, I thought they might be a better fit for me. Any couple should look well matched, don't you think? Yes, some websites did raise yellow flags, warning that the breed's energy needed to be carefully channeled. I felt that for me, this meant buying an Arabian would be like buying a playful yet extremely loyal, Jack Russell terrier dog, and I was OK with that.

To be perfectly honest, when I had sought Tom's advice about what type of horse to buy, he suggested a well-trained quarter horse about twelve years old and with lots of trail experience. He knew I wanted to do more trail riding, and he thought an older quarter horse would do the trick. Funny, but his suggestion immediately saddened me. Deep down, I knew he meant well, but buying an older horse seemed to me like buying an adult dog when what I really wanted was a young pup of a horse that I could bond with. Bear, my beloved miniature schnauzer, was almost thirteen now. I could see he was becoming feebler day by day. The thought of losing him and not being able to cuddle his warm body in my arms anymore had been tugging at my heartstrings. I somehow couldn't bear the thought of buying a middle-aged horse and maybe only having it for ten or fifteen years.

One day, just as we were finishing up one of my regular riding lessons, I decided to broach the subject with Tom. "What do you think about me buying a younger horse?"

"Well, if you buy a younger horse, you're going to have to invest a lot of time and effort training him. Sure, younger horses are less expensive, but that's because they are untrained. It costs a lot to train a horse, and it takes time and patience."

"If I bought a young horse, couldn't you train him for me?"

"Yes, I could. But you're going to have to do a lot of groundwork first. You may not be able to ride him for quite a few months after getting him."

"I don't mind that. I'm going to have the horse for the rest of its life. A few months of waiting won't hurt me. Do you think I could handle it, Tom? Do you think I'm a good enough rider?"

"Yes, you're a good enough rider, but training a horse is a big challenge."

Given we were already on the subject of horse selection, I'd boldly asked, "What do you think of Arabians?"

A long silence on Tom's part followed while he looked down at the arena floor and began making patterns in the dust with his right foot. Finally, he said, "Hmmm, they're OK." I could tell by his response that an Arabian was not top of his list as a good choice for me. He then went on to explain, "Arabians are what you call a hot horse. They are a little flighty, and some of them—not all—are just nuts. I've trained a few, and they are a handful."

"But they're just so pretty!" I added with a laugh.

"Yah, they're pretty...pretty crazy!" he replied with a chuckle.

Given Tom's barn was filled with quarter horses, it seemed clear he was a real quarter-horse kind of guy, so I chalked up his comments to more of a personal preference—just as some people love Saint Bernard dogs while others love pointers. In truth, I don't really know what possessed me, but I completely ignored Tom's prudent advice. So as choice and stupidity would have it, within a few weeks, I'd purchased a completely untrained, gorgeous three-year-old Arabian horse that I found in Langley, British Columbia (just a border crossing away from our house). Looking back, I distinctly remember a twinge of regret and nervousness deep down in my stomach as I signed the purchase contract. But then I said to myself, "Don't worry; everyone is nervous when they buy their first horse. It'll be fine. It'll all work itself out." I should have listened to that basic gut instinct.

When the horse trailer pulled up to the veterinary inspection station of the customs office, I took my umbrella and ran out in the rain to say hello to the sellers. As I approached the trailer, I couldn't see my horse, as all the trailer windows were shut. It was clear to everyone in the area, however, that there was a horse inside. Yes, *my* horse was quite methodically kicking the back door of the trailer—*bam, bam, bam* was the sound of hoof against metal. The sellers quickly herded me back into the customs office, where we waited for the inspector to get back with his report. When the vet finished inspecting the horse, he stamped the paperwork saying the horse had passed the inspection. As he handed me the certificate, he didn't mention the kicking. He just looked at me and grinned. "He sure is pretty!"

I ran to my car and pulled up in front of the horse trailer to lead the sellers to Tom's barn. Now back on the Washington side of the border, we followed the quiet country roads toward the town of Blaine. Just as we got underway, it started raining cats and dogs, which was a little unusual, for Washington State is better known for weeks of dreary drizzle rather than torrential rains. Alone in my car, I could only hear two things: my windshield wipers furiously trying to keep up with the rain and the muffled sound of a horse kicking inside the trailer following me. I couldn't help thinking, *And this is supposed to be one of the happiest days of my life! Hmmm...hope it's not a bad omen!*

When we finally arrived at the Peace Arch Equestrian Center, the sellers led my new horse into the arena to let him unwind a bit from the long ride. We all watched as this magnificent-looking Arabian bucked, snorted, performed the most extended, lofty trot I'd ever seen, stopped, jumped up into an elevated levade, and then continued running. His pace began to quicken with each circling of the arena, and soon he was in a flat-out gallop. Just as I thought the horse might explode like a wind-up toy, he did it! *My new horse fell right on his head!* Yes, he had tripped over his two front feet, summersaulted forward onto his head and back, somehow jumped back up with the athleticism of a gymnast, and continued running. It was as if he had said, "You didn't see that. No, not me! I didn't fall!"

I stood there watching him in awe, wonder, and utter fear.

Carlene, Tom's wife, joined me at the side of the arena. She knew how much I had wanted a horse, and she congratulated me on my purchase. "So, what's his name?"

"Merlot...I decided to call him Merlot, like the wine."

"That's a nice name, and he is a really beautiful red bay. I think he's cute!" she said enthusiastically.

He certainly is a handsome horse, I thought. His solid, red bay coat gleamed with health and was elegantly framed by a long, flowing black mane and tail. His well-shaped black hooves were strong and sturdy, and they propelled him quickly forward with the bounce and agility of a ballet dancer. Like a young teenage boy, he hadn't finished growing yet and was still a little on the slim side, but I knew he would fill out later.

Tom had been running some errands and arrived back at the barn shortly after the sellers left. "So, this is your new horse!" Tom said as he leaned his arms against the top rung of the arena fence and looked Merlot over carefully.

"Tom," I said in all seriousness, "I'm a little nervous. Do you mind walking him to his stall for me?"

"No problem," he replied.

Back in his stall, Merlot resumed his agitated circling. By now, he was sweating in a panic and jumping from one side of the stall to the other. Within minutes, the stall I had meticulously cleaned that same morning became strewn with nervous poops, and shavings were flying every which way. The water dish quickly became littered with shavings, but

I certainly wasn't going to venture into the stall to clean it. Although the stall fronts were quite high, they didn't have bars on them, and I began to worry that Merlot would try to jump out. I suddenly had visions of him launching himself perilously onto the stall divider in the middle of the night and dying a tragic, untimely death.

Tom was standing beside me and, sensing my fear and concern, tried to be reassuring. "Don't worry, Dagny. He'll settle down. By tomorrow, you'll see, he'll be much better." *Yes,* I thought, *if he survives the night and doesn't commit suicide.*

It was just at that moment that Kam arrived. He had come straight from work and looked quite handsome walking down the barn aisle in his white dress shirt, black slacks, and nicely polished shoes. At six feet tall, Kam towers over me. While in high school, his hair had been solid black; it was now fringed with gray, giving him a rather distinguished look, like a male model in a Lands' End catalog. Trying not to get his clothes dirty, he was walking toward me in the dead center of the barn aisle while deliberately trying to avoid any encounter with the sawdust-covered barn dog. After looking at Merlot from a suitable distance, Kam gave me a big hug and said, "So, congratulations! Are you excited?"

Trying to hide the anxiety that was now rushing through every vein in my body, I mustered up the most convincing "Yes, I'm so happy! Thank you so much!" that I could. As I left the barn, I thought, *Oh, God, what have I gotten myself into?* At that moment, I remembered that a friend of mine once told me, "Life is not pink!" Yes, sometimes we humans take steps to complicate our lives and mess things up a little.

Owners of new puppies might relate to my situation. There is that virgin excitement you feel when you're at the dog breeder's home, most likely sitting on the kitchen floor, with shiny new puppies climbing all over you. And even though you know you will have to shell out money for vet bills and dog chow for the next twelve to fifteen years, you justify the purchase in your mind, saying it'll all be worth it—*I mean, puppies are just so adorable!* Then, depending on your own temperament, you select either the most handsome puppy, the most gregarious puppy, or perhaps the quiet runt of the litter that seems like it could use a break in life. Picking that squiggly puppy up into your hands, you smell its warm, milky breath, and then you're a complete goner. You grab your pen, sign the deposit check, and make a life commitment.

A few weeks later, you return to the breeders for your little bundle of love. Arriving home with that eight-week-old puppy, you stand in awe when the very first thing it does is shit on your floor and start chewing on the nearest table leg. Yes, it's only then, and with the first doleful howls that keep you up all night, that a twinge of regret may seep into your consciousness.

That night, as I lay in bed anxiously thinking about the day's events and wondering what lay in store for me, Merlot became my brand-new puppy.

11

Young Wine Can Be Sour

As it turns out, Merlot wasn't the best name for my new horse. He wasn't a fine, red wine to be savored. Truly, a better use for that vintage would have been in a crushing blow against the side of a ship. I should have called him Napoleon, for the horse consistently demonstrated a strong desire for world domination. In fact, during our first six months together, I often called him "Evil Demon" and "Son of a #$%!"

After my childhood dream tried to bite me on two separate occasions, I began questioning all references to Arabian loyalty. Our first months together were filled with anxiety and fear. Some days it was his anxiety and fear, and some days it was mine. After one particularly difficult day, I walked up to Evil Demon's stall and yelled, "You know, you're still on probation! I could send you back or make dog food out of you!"

He glanced over at me in his haughty way as if to say, "If you don't have carrots, I don't have anything to say to you!" Yes, it was on day two of our bad marriage (Merlot and I had skipped the honeymoon stage) that I realized that food was the only thing this horse liked.

Still my number-one cheerleader, Mom greeted me at the barn all smiles the day after Merlot arrived, toting a gift bucket full of new horse brushes and horse treats. You see, she was a "grand dam" now and had to spoil her "grandpony." Now in her early seventies, retirement life suited my mother. She seemed calmer of late and more settled in her own skin. For about a year, she had been renting an apartment in the town of Chilliwack, BC. Thankfully, she no longer had the energy to move about from one city to another or one house to another. Whenever she got itchy feet these days, she limited herself to rearranging the furniture.

I noticed Mom seemed to be shrinking of late. She had become a tad shorter and a little fluffy. For her age, however, she was still quite vibrant, and her piercing blue eyes always shined brightly from her time-weathered face. Her hair, still cropped short, had lost all memory of its steely gray and was now pure white, surprisingly thick and soft. She arrived at the barn early that day, and after giving me a big hug and an "I'm so happy for you!" we both tentatively petted Merlot's head while feeding him horse treats. It seemed if we were offering treats, Merlot would tolerate our presence. When not being fed, he would aggressively pin his ears at us and at anyone who had the nerve to pass his stall.

Having only worked with gentle, well-trained school horses my entire riding life, Merlot's behavior was unnerving, to say the least. Taking a deep breath, I decided to venture into his stall and start the all-important bonding process. Like a scene from a girlie horse movie, I was sure that after a few wary moments, Merlot would look into my soul and understand I was good and kind, walk up to me, gently smell my hand, and all would be well. Unfortunately, Merlot had not read the same script. Or maybe he had just finished reading *The Exorcist*. For as soon as I slid the door open, he swung his rear toward the door and threatened to kick my head in. My response was, "Holy shit!" as I quickly slammed the door shut. Tom just happened to be walking by the stall when I exclaimed, "Tom! Merlot turned his backside toward me when I opened his stall door!"

Tom stopped a moment to glance into the stall and said, "Yup...I can see that." Merlot had not budged and was still standing in the same spot, his butt toward the door, ready to battle anyone who dared cross the threshold. After a few minutes of silence, Tom turned to walk away, saying, "I'll fix that;

don't worry. Come back in a few days." Relieved to know there was someone I could count on to help, I took Tom's advice and returned to check on the horse's progress a few days later.

Returning the following Wednesday, I found Merlot not in his stall but tied to a big post against the arena wall. Merlot, obviously miffed at being tied, was rather forcefully pawing the ground in front of him. Balancing himself on three legs, he was pounding his right front leg into the arena sand as if trying to crush a foe. I left the horse in the arena and searched the barn for Tom, finally finding him in the small, commercial trailer at the front of the building that functioned as his office. Tom was on the phone, ordering a load of hay and various supplements, so while I waited, I perused a shelf full of dusty horse manuals that were stacked at the far end of the trailer.

In line with horse-barn decorating standards, the walls of the office were lined with faded horse-show ribbons, yellowing pictures of first and favorite horses, and shelves of dusty trophies. Wood-engraved horse humor added a finishing touch to the room: "Talk to the hoof," "The barn was clean yesterday. Wish you were here!" and my favorite, "Gone riding, be back *maybe*." The office also featured another horse-barn staple—a coffee machine only capable of producing what I refer to as industrial-grade coffee, the stock powdered creamer, sugar packets, and questionably clean coffee mugs.

When Tom's call finally ended, I asked, "Hey Tom, I was just wondering, why is Merlot tied in the arena?"

Tom, swiveling his chair to face me while holding a warm cup of coffee in one hand, replied, "He has to learn patience."

"Too funny!" I said with a laugh. "How long has he been there?"

Tom took a sip of his coffee, and then looking at his watch, he said with a grin, "Oh, about two hours now. Is he still pawing the ground?"

"Yes," I replied. "He's digging a hole to China."

"Too bad. I won't untie him until he stops pawing."

I thought it was hysterical, and glad to see someone was up to the task of tough love. Returning to the arena, I stuck my head through the fence and looked at Merlot from a distance. "Are you learning patience there, my boy?" I said with a snicker.

Merlot stopped for a moment to pin his ears back at me as if to say, "Buzz off!" and went back to pawing.

I just shook my head and went home laughing. "Goodness, what a horse I have!"

Within a week, Tom solved the Evil Demon's "I will kick all who enter stall" behavior. I'm not sure how this feat was accomplished, but I was grateful for the change. As if on cue, now when I opened the door, Merlot quickly and dutifully turned to face it. It seemed Merlot had got an ass-kicking himself and was now committed to responding appropriately to visitors.

While Tom was using his own tried-and-true training methods, I, not having any training methods to speak of, thought I could use food to wiggle my way into Merlot's heart. Since I always arrived at his stall with a handful of fresh, peeled, washed, and sliced carrots, Merlot quickly developed a Pavlovian association between me and food. Tom, catching me in the act one day, cautioned, "You know, feeding him carrots won't teach that horse to respect you."

"Yeah, but I'm hoping he'll at least start to like me," I replied.

Tom shook his head, and looking down at the carrots in my hand, he said in disbelief, "Did you actually cut the heads off those carrots, peel, and slice them for the horse?"

"Yes," I replied sheepishly.

"You do realize he's a horse and not a human, don't you?" Tom laughed.

"Yes, I *do*!" I blushed.

Apart from his daily training sessions with Tom, Merlot spent his day in a stall, and that couldn't be easy for a young horse. Determined to give him more exercise, I thought I would get up early and let Merlot run around the arena before the lesson day started. After spending years working in barns, bringing horses to and from pastures all day long, I couldn't believe I was stressing over the thought of trying to get my horse from his stall and down about fifty feet of barn aisle to the indoor arena. Like a person who has been in a car accident who becomes paralyzed with fear when sitting behind the wheel, in less than a few weeks, Merlot's antics had completely eroded my confidence.

After one fitful night's sleep, I eventually decided on a plan of attack and executed it perfectly. The next morning, I entered Merlot's stall with carrots and quickly threw them in his feed bucket to distract him while I put his halter on. Shaking like a leaf, I tried to hide my fear by whispering sweet nothings in his ears as I carefully wrapped the halter around his head. Waiting quietly at his side until he finished all the carrots, I slowly led him out of his stall, down the aisle, and into the arena. Turning him toward me before I let him loose, I nervously unlatched his halter. Merlot jumped like a coiled spring into the air, spent a good minute bucking and kicking, and then took off in a ground-covering extended trot, his head and tail arched stiffly in the air. I hurried to take cover and watched in amazement. Upon reaching the first corner, Merlot stopped, spun around, and, prancing in place, uttered loud, ungodly sounding snorts and blows with his nose that made him appear more like a fire-breathing dragon than a horse. The running, spinning, and snort-and-blow continued for a good ten minutes until he finally stopped, dropped down onto his back, and began rolling with glee in the arena dust.

It was just then that Tom, arriving early at the barn to feed the horses, joined me at the side of the arena, holding a big mug of morning java in his hand. "Well, looks like Merlot is having fun," he said quietly.

"Yes," I replied. "He certainly blew off some steam…but, Tom, I forgot one thing."

"What's that?"

"How on earth do I catch him?"

"Well, just go in there and put his halter on him."

Seriously? I thought. *He expects me to get in the ring with that wild beast?* But, too embarrassed to say anything, after a few moments of hesitation, I grabbed the halter and lead rope off the fence and opened the arena gate, carefully closing it behind me. My heart pounding, I walked toward Merlot, who was eyeing me with a most mischievous look in his eye. As soon as I got within thirty feet of him, he took off like a shot to the other side of the arena, throwing in a few bucks along the way for good measure. Turning toward Tom, I pleaded, "So what do I do now?"

"Here, take this whip," Tom said as he motioned me over to the fence to take a long longe whip that he handed me. *Oh, God*, I thought, *surely he is not going to ask me to beat the horse.* "Now hold the whip up in your hand and walk toward him. This time, make him run away from you."

"Really, you want me to make the horse run away from me? That's how I'm supposed to catch him?"

"Yup."

"OK," I said with disbelief in my voice. I walked toward Merlot, and seeing me walking toward him with the whip, he trotted away from me. "So, what do I do now, Tom?"

"Keep following him with the whip, and make him move."

So, like a shepherd herding sheep, I kept after Merlot as he whizzed around me. Even when the horse tried to deke me out with a change of direction, I continued walking toward him, making him trot and canter away from me. "Now," explained Tom, "Drop your whip, say 'Whoa,' and walk up to him to put the halter on."

By this time, Merlot had worked up a sweat and was huffing and puffing, his nostrils expanding and contracting with every breath. To my surprise, he stood quietly and let me halter him without a fuss. "Wow, that actually worked!"

"Yes. That's because horses are lazy, and all that running around is hard work. As soon as Merlot realized running away wasn't really working for him but was making him work harder, he decided on an easier solution, which was to stop and let you halter him. Every time he takes off on you, make him move. You do that one or two times, and he'll understand running away doesn't work. He'll learn to stand still when you go get him."

I looked at Merlot, who was standing quietly beside me, his head lowered, catching his breath. "You hear that, Merlot?" I said with a laugh as I petted him on his neck. "You'll actually *learn* things around here!"

Like a parent whose three-year-old finally uses the potty, I was really encouraged by this small training success and left the barn that day full of hope. And, like that same parent, having glimpsed the light at the end of the diaper tunnel, I was equally discouraged when faced with the next shitty experience.

It happened a few days later, when I innocently tied Merlot to a post in the arena and started to groom him. Evil Demon wouldn't let me pick up his front feet to clean them, and I was too scared to go anywhere near his back legs. *Well,* I said to myself, *we can work on feet cleaning later.* I picked up a dandy brush and started brushing his mane. Unlike every other horse I had known, Merlot didn't seem to like being brushed at all. In fact, the whole process seemed to irritate him to no end. *Hmmm…maybe his skin is more sensitive to these bristles.* So I switched to a softer body brush.

Just as I was brushing his midsection, he suddenly swung his head around to bite me. His teeth hit my arm, but he didn't get ahold of me. With lightning-fast reflex, my instinctive response was to take the brush, which I was holding in my left hand, wind it up like a baseball bat, and swing it at him with all my might. Giving him a good wallop on his side, I then stepped back to yell, "You son of a #$%!" We both stood there, shocked and trembling. Merlot was as surprised at my response as I was. Leaving the horse in the arena, I ran and got Tom. Tom calmly untied Merlot and then aggressively made the horse walk backward, clear across the arena. This seemed to put the Evil Demon in a more polite frame of mind.

As Tom retied Merlot to the wall, I said, almost in tears, "And he won't let me pick his feet!" Without a word, Tom grabbed the hoof pick and cleaned Merlot's feet. The horse picked up his feet politely for Tom, not giving him a moment's grief.

"Now," Tom said, "When you're grooming this horse, keep a close eye on his head with the corner of your eye. If he ever tries that again, as he turns his head to bite you, without looking directly at him, use your elbow to 'accidentally' hit him right in the nose with it."

"So you're telling me you want me to use my elbow to bash him in the nose, but I shouldn't look him directly in the eye when I do it?" I asked, not quite believing what I was hearing.

"Yup. What you want him to think is, 'Whenever I try to bite her, it hurts my nose.'"

"Why shouldn't I look directly at him?" I asked.

"When you look directly at him, that's more aggressive to the horse. You want him to think he hurt his nose by trying to bite you, that it was all his doing. You get him good once or twice, he'll never, ever try it again."

On the one hand, I was deeply upset and not sure I could execute the plan, but on the other hand, there was a small part of me that was actually hoping he would try it again and I could nail the little bugger. Well, Evil Demon didn't let me down. A few days later, during another grooming session, he tried to bite me. This time, watching his head from the corner of my eye, I was ready, and as he swung his head around to bite, my elbow swung equally fast right into his nose. The elbow hook worked like a charm, and yes, Arabians are smart. He never tried it again!

Poor Tom. The next few months were filled with the many "won'ts" he had to fix. "Tom, Merlot won't go into the wash stall…Merlot won't let me get near him with the hose…Merlot won't let me put his blanket on him…Merlot won't let me touch his ears…Merlot is freaking out at the sound of the clippers…Merlot almost trampled me when he spooked at a garbage bag…Merlot kicked a horse that walked by him in the barn aisle…Merlot is still pinning his ears at anyone who walks by his stall…Merlot attacked a dog that wandered into the arena…Tom, I just saw Merlot stomp a snake to death in the pasture…"

Yes, I apparently owned the barn bully, and Merlot's thirst for world domination included humans, horses, small mammals, and reptiles. Although Tom trained Merlot to stand still for grooming and pick up his feet properly, the horse still seemed utterly miffed every single time I tried to groom him.

After two months with my new steed, this was my professional clinical assessment of the horse:

- Likes: food, bucking, galloping, rolling in dust
- Dislikes: everything else in the world
- Observations: anger management issues (with tendency to kick first, ask questions later)
- Potential for Improvement: to be determined

Like a depressed parent who recognizes her beloved child is a little menace but just doesn't feel up to a fight, by month three, I took the easy route and began focusing on Merlot's likes, giving him ample treats and free time in the arena (for all the running and bucking he dearly loved). My routine involved arriving at the barn by 6:30 a.m. and, after his carrot appetizer, letting him loose. I would then ascend a flight of wooden stairs that led to a small viewing area overlooking the arena. Invariably, the barn's cat would follow me up the stairs, and first brushing her body against my leg, eventually leap into my lap, purring for attention. Although I'm quite allergic to cats, I couldn't resist this cat's friendliness, and it was nice to have a little company while I watched my horse's antics below. The speed with which Merlot galloped, bucked, and spun about the arena just blew my mind. Day after day of watching him, I kept wondering if I too would be catapulted from that upwardly mobile back of his.

Finally, hoping to get words of wisdom from the Arabian community, I posted the following on the Arabian Horse Forum:

> I recently bought my first horse—an Arabian gelding and untrained three-year-old. There are times when I look at the horse and wonder, will he ever be calm? Did I buy a horse that is too hot? Did I buy the right breed, or are Arabians just nuts? I ponder this question as I watch him every day in the arena,

bucking and running with lots of snort and blow. Just watching him makes me nervous. I keep thinking that one day when I start to ride him, he will start bucking the same way. I wanted the experience of a young horse and am certainly getting it, but boy, oh boy, on a daily basis, it is not easy. He is a headstrong, dominant type. He's getting sixty days of professional training, so I'm sure that will help, but if anyone would like to share their "I had a crazy Arabian who is now calm" story, I would love to hear it. Or maybe some Arabians are just nuts, and you have some words or wisdom for coping? Thanks in advance.

I got some response posts:

—Ah yes, I read your post with laughter. Yes, I remember those days! Dancer is twenty-four now...The long and short—*yes, yes, yes*, he will calm down. My opinion—eight is the magic number. Your horse will calm down a bunch then, but at some point, between the seventh and eighth year, Dancer turned a major corner...

Oh, that's just peachy, I thought. *Merlot is only three, and I have to wait until he is eight to calm down?*

> —I have a four-year-old purebred Arab. If he gets any calmer, he'll be dead. Started out that way and has always been that way. It isn't the breed; it's the individual. I do think as young horses go, mine is the exception to the rule. So, yes, yours will more than likely calm down. It's a wonder what a professional trainer can get done in sixty to ninety days.

Great, I thought, *it's the individual. I picked a psycho Arab when there are nice ones out there.*

> —If watching your horse run and buck in the arena makes you nervous, stop watching.

Finally, a practical suggestion!

From that day forward, I never watched Merlot in the arena. Instead, after letting him loose, I would walk up and down the barn aisle, petting the friendly school horses while trying to ignore the ominous sounds of bucks, squeals, and galloping feet in the arena.

I began to get a real sense that Merlot has what one calls a "strong personality" when the equine dentist came out to the barn to float his teeth. You see, a horse's teeth need to be filed down, usually once a year, to make sure there are no sharp points that might cause the horse pain when he holds a bit in his mouth or when he is eating. Tom suggested it would be a good idea to float Merlot's teeth before his first bridling experience. Given his normally angry personality, I didn't even want to imagine what Merlot would be like if he was actually in pain, so I quickly agreed and scheduled the procedure.

After sedating a horse, an equine dentist puts a metal speculum into the horse's mouth that mechanically wedges it open. The brace looks rather Frankensteinish, but when you think about it, how else are you going to get the horse's mouth to stay open? Equine dentists then use a simple metal rasp to file down the teeth. Some dentists prefer using an electric rasp, which looks like a drill bit with a long shaft that has a long, flat spinning head that files the teeth down. The whole procedure usually only takes a half hour, and the horse is sedated the whole time, so it is relatively pain-free—although I'm sure after the sedation wears off, a horse might wonder why its teeth ache a bit.

When the day came for Merlot's procedure, I can't say I was surprised when he reared up aggressively as the vet tried to sedate him. With Tom's help, the vet eventually got the needle in. When the dentist tried to put the speculum on his head, Merlot, who should have been well sedated by this time, put up a pretty impressive fight, backing up quickly and dislodging the speculum from his head, throwing it onto the ground. The vet then gave him a second needle. On the second attempt at putting the speculum on, Merlot wasn't able to rear up but still managed a swift kick with his left hind leg that was aimed rather strategically at the vet standing beside him. The vet, who jumped out of the way in time, stood there shaking his head. "I don't believe it. That last shot should have knocked him out cold!" In the end, the amount of sedation they had to give Merlot could have taken out a rhino. Yes, my boy was certainly willing to put up a good fight.

Understandably, there were days I wanted to throw in the towel, but I tried to focus on Merlot's good qualities. He was certainly a pretty horse. His feet were of excellent quality, and he exuded good health. The vet even commented that he had superb teeth. The horse was a perfect size for me, not too big, not too small, and he certainly wasn't a picky eater. To top it off, he had pretty brown eyes, excellent conformation, and really smooth gaits. These are all fine traits in a horse. My only real problem was that he needed a lobotomy.

12

A Fence Comes Down

Roller coasters can be pretty scary. And then there is that moment, at the pinnacle of the first drop, when you let out that hair-raising scream as you realize you no longer have control over *anything*! Well, this was one of those days.

It was a Saturday that started out pleasant and promising, as most Saturdays do. We were now into our second fall season in Washington State, and I had noticed a few red leaves peeping through the green fir trees. In our backyard, the Japanese maples glistened and shimmered with morning dew while the leaves of many birch trees had already turned a wet, pale yellow and started falling onto the lawn. Heavier vests and warmer pants had found their way to the top drawers of our bureaus, ready to protect us from the damp cold. Indeed, I now had a decent collection of corduroy pants, fleece, and rain breakers to get through the winter. Although the temperatures here in Washington State never dipped anywhere near Quebec's minus twenty-two Fahrenheit, I still hadn't decided which type of winter I liked better—freezing cold and sunny (à la Quebec) or mild cold and damp (à la Washington State). This particular Saturday was quite nippy, so that morning, we turned on the gas fireplace to get the damp chill out of the house.

Kam took lessons with Tom on Saturdays, so after a leisurely breakfast and a few slowly sipped coffees by the fire, we made our way to the barn. I helped Kam tack up Domino, his regular school horse, and watched as Tom started teaching Kam his lesson. On the way into the barn, I had noticed there were no horses turned out in the back pasture, so I asked Tom if it was OK to put Merlot there. My confidence to at least walk my new horse around the premises had grown in recent weeks, so I felt up to the task of at least turning him out on my own. Tom said, "Sure, OK," and went back to teaching Kam.

After indulging Merlot with a few equine cookies (yes, there are companies that make cookies just for horses!), I innocently led him to the back pasture. The grass was tall and wet and, although littered with the yellow leaves of fall in some areas, the pasture still looked green and tasty. I was sure

Merlot would enjoy the smorgasbord in front of him. After leading him, I safely closed the gate, turning Merlot to face me before removing his halter. Rather than shoving his nose into the deep, green grass and gobbling away as I had expected, Merlot took off at a flat run as if I had just let him free on the plains of Nebraska. The pasture was about an acre in size and bordered with a thick, white ribbon of electric fence. Within five seconds, Merlot had covered so much ground, I realized he wasn't going to stop when he hit the electric wire. He ran through the white electric tape, but instead of breaking, the tape stayed wrapped around his neck as he pulled. The metal fence posts started toppling like dominoes as Merlot, now utterly panicked at this white wire "chasing" him, began running toward the road and oncoming traffic.

I stood paralyzed with fear and just watched as my horse charged full throttle toward a busy street. *Oh my God,* I thought, *he is going to run into a car or cause an accident and kill someone. God help me, please!* The horse was running so fast, I knew I couldn't make it to the street before he did, so there was no chance I could head him off. I then did the only thing I could think of and let out the aforementioned hair-raising scream—"*Tom!*"

It was just at that moment that Merlot, by some miracle, changed course and started barreling back toward me. He ran past the open back door of the barn, forcing me to jump over the snaking electric wire, as he had effectively galloped a wide circle around me. He was running so fast, he skidded on the gravel as he rounded the first corner of the barn and ran along the outside wall of the arena toward the front of the building. I took off at a run through the center barn aisle and, reaching the halfway point, glanced to my right to see that Kam had dismounted and was standing safely beside his horse in the middle of the arena. I continued running down the aisle toward the front of the barn, only to come to a screeching stop myself as I realized there was wire about two feet off the ground strung across the entire length of the barn door opening. Jumping over the wire, I couldn't see a horse in either direction, so I followed the wire toward the left corner of the barn and, as I came around it, saw that Tom had managed to corral Merlot into a pen.

The horse was completely frazzled. The situation was extremely dangerous for both Tom and the horse, as Merlot was jumping around wildly. The wire tape had somehow got itself wrapped around Merlot's neck several times, and some of the wire was even tangled around his front legs. Tom entered the pen and after closing the gate behind him, calmly approached the horse. Talking to him softly and quietly, Tom slowly unwrapped the wire from around Merlot's head. "Whoa, boy, you're OK. You got yourself into a mess now, didn't ya? Whoa, stand still now, there you go…" I stood outside the pen and just watched wordlessly, as I didn't want to say or do anything that would further aggravate the situation. Every nerve in that horse's body was taut, and he looked like he would explode at any minute, but he let Tom remove the tape. After getting all the wire off, Tom left the pen and locked Merlot in it. "Leave him in there for a while, Dagny, till he calms down."

Tom needn't have worried. Merlot was still quivering and wide-eyed, and I wasn't about to step anywhere near that animal. "Oh my God, Tom, I'm so sorry! I never thought he would take down the fence! He was running so fast, I'm not even sure if he saw the wire! Maybe he doesn't know what an electric fence is?"

"No, I guess he doesn't," said Tom, handing me the bundle of wire in his hands.

"Will Merlot be OK? Should I call the vet?" I asked, as Merlot appeared to have rope-type burns on his neck and legs.

"No, he'll be fine. He just rubbed some hair off," Tom replied as he walked back toward the arena to finish Kam's lesson. While Tom seemed unfazed, I was completely unglued and shaking like a leaf. In less than ten minutes, my horse had taken an acre of fencing down and wrapped a quite sizable barn like a spool with electric tape!

I began gathering up the wire and had just freed the front door of the barn when a car pulled up with a young family in it. The father got out, and gathering up a baby from a baby seat, he was joined by his wife and a beautiful, young daughter who looked to be about six years old. "Hello!" they said warmly. "Our little girl here," said the father proudly while gently caressing the back of her little blond head, "wants to take riding lessons, and we thought we would come by and talk to the owner. Do they give lessons here?"

I just stood and stared blankly at the four of them, thinking, *Oh my God! What would have happened if they had arrived ten minutes earlier? Merlot could have trampled them or strangled them with the wire, or he might have careened right to avoid them and run into traffic on the side street!* Eventually pulling myself out of my blank stare, I replied distractedly, "Yeah lessons...umm...the owner is giving one now, and he can talk to you when he's done." Placing the bundle of wire that I had in my hands down on the ground to the left of the front door, I led the young family to the arena and told them to wait for Tom. Then I climbed up the stairs to the observation deck to pull myself together. The terrifying scenes that had just unfolded were swirling through my mind so quickly, I felt sure I was going to throw up.

Suddenly, I heard purring, and the barn kitty jumped up onto the bench beside me and started rubbing her whiskers against my arm. I couldn't hold back the tears that began streaming down my face. Placing the cat on my lap, I stroked her soft fur as I thought of the horrors that could have been. I don't consider myself terribly religious, but I thanked God over and over, gently rubbing the back of the kitty's head as she purred contentedly.

There have been other moments in my life when I've been on the right side of fate. Indeed, I suspect many of us humans experience near misses once in a while. I remember how I once accidentally drove the wrong way down a one-way street and, by the grace of God, managed a screeching U-turn before the oncoming traffic reached me. Of course, I'll never forget the time I was hiking down a steep mountain ridge with Kam. He had climbed down the ridge first and was ahead of and below me when I accidentally dislodged a large, flat rock with my foot. The rock, which was more like a one-foot-wide slab, careened through the air and narrowly missed crushing Kam's skull by but a few inches. I remember then too I was paralyzed with fear and only had time for a few Hail Marys as I watched the rock fly in slow motion toward him. Sometimes we humans are just plain lucky.

As Kam's lesson was wrapping up, I picked up the kitty and placed her gingerly on the floor. As I walked slowly down the steps back to the arena, I made a solemn promise to start praying to God on a nonemergency basis—as it seemed a bit selfish on my part to only call his name at times of dire need. I suddenly had this vision of God looking down upon me, scowling and shaking his head, saying, "Sure, you don't stop by my house anymore or even ring me on the phone, but the moment something scares the bejesus out of you, you start screaming, 'God help me!'"

Kam was leading Domino out of the arena when he stopped to say to me, "Boy, that was something else! I'm just having my lesson when suddenly, I hear you scream. Tom told me to get off Domino, and I had just dismounted when we saw Merlot run by the arena with all this stuff streaming behind him. My horse got a little freaked out, but luckily I was already on the ground and was able to control him. Tom told me to stay put when he ran off to help you...Dagny, he told me what happened. What a nut bar that horse is!"

"Kam, we were so lucky no one was hurt," I said gravely, wiping the last sign of tears from my cheeks.

"Are you sure you want to keep him?" Kam said in all seriousness while looking deeply into my eyes, trying to gauge how I felt about the incident.

"Well, it wasn't really the horse's fault. I don't think he saw the wire. Or maybe he was never in electric fencing before?" I knew deep down, Kam wanted me to ditch the horse, but he wasn't going to press the matter. He would let that be my decision.

Kam and I were both silent on the way home in the car, each of us deep in thought, but our dog Bear's greeting as we opened the garage door made us both smile. With age, Bear's separation anxiety had worsened. Now, when we left him alone for even a few hours, Bear frantically screeched with joy upon our return. When we opened the door between the garage and the house, he put his front paws on my legs while furiously wagging his stubby little tail. By the way he acted, you'd think I'd just saved him from a sinking ship. Leaning over, I picked the dog up in my arms and pressed his little gray beard to my cheek. "Now, *you've* never given me any real trouble, have you, Bear," I said, squeezing the dog's warm body tighter in my arms. "Yes, when you were a pup, you did chew some table legs, and there were a few carpet accidents we don't want to talk about, but at least I never had to worry about you trampling people or potentially killing others in a traffic accident!" As if to console me, Bear gently rested his bearded muzzle on my shoulder while Kam petted his head and ears. Putting the dog back down on the floor, we went about the evening as usual.

When I went to bed that night, I took a moment to look out of the bedroom window and up at the stars. There was a bit of cloud cover that night, but as the clouds blew quietly through the night sky, I could see stars twinkling peacefully above. I let out a deep sigh, and as I climbed into bed, I noticed a deep sense of gratitude had settled into my heart. Before falling off to sleep, I remembered my promise to God and whispered a most sincere "Our Father, who art in heaven."

The next day, I found Tom out in the pasture, restaking the fence line. He had already purchased a new spool of electric tape and was hammering in the metal posts with a fencepost driver. I apologized profusely and offered to help or pay for the new wire.

"Don't worry about it," Tom said as he continued hammering in the posts. "That's just horses." He never said another word or complained about all the extra work he had to do on account of Merlot's mayhem. As I walked back toward the barn, I thought, *Now, that is a good man. He didn't have to be so gracious.*

Arriving at Merlot's stall, I looked in and said, "You know, Merlot, you really are a complete nut job!"

Merlot looked at me with his piercing eyes as if to say, "It wasn't me—it was *all your fault*! First, you let me free, and I'm just having a good run when I get electrocuted, and then these white snakes come out of nowhere! They were making terrible hissing sounds and flying everywhere, chasing me! What kind of a pasture is that to put a horse in?" Yes, there are always two sides to every story.

Time away from the barn seemed just what the doctor ordered, so during the next few days, I devoted myself to mentally calming activities like cleaning the garage and re-organizing sock drawers. I quite liked our Washington home. It was a lovely, one-story bungalow that backed onto the ninth hole of a golf course. The community, named Semiahmoo, caters to golfers and retirees, and I think Kam and I were probably one of the youngest couples in the neighborhood at the time. Copious amounts of rain meant all the homes had lush gardens, and one would think, driving around the community's streets (which had all been named after birds), that each homeowner was in competition with the next over who had the prettier garden. Yes, it seemed I was living in a residential version of Butchart Gardens. In the spring and summer, rhododendrons and azaleas held center stage while tall, green pines formed a lovely backdrop to flowering cherry and magnolia trees. Roses of every color delighted the eyes and scented the air, competing only with bushy lilacs for attention. Determined to impress all passers-by, homeowners, or rather their well-paid landscapers, had underplanted even their plainest trees with tulips, lily of the valley, crocuses, and heathers.

That week as I weeded our garden, I thought, *Yes, the rainy Northwest does have its charms.* A solid week of heavy-duty housecleaning and yard maintenance had cleared my mind, and I felt ready to face any mayhem Merlot might kick my way. Yes, a week of sheer manual labor is often a cure for all one's worries. My mood had improved. I was even feeling undaunted by the fungus threatening our roses and was determined to find environmentally friendly ways to capture the many slugs that slithered around the house.

We lived on a street called Bald Eagle Drive but had made friends with neighbors on Canvasback, Osprey Road, and Peregrine Way. Sure enough, I once saw a bald eagle soar above our street, and canvasback ducks were nesting in the reeds along the nearby bay. I was still on the lookout for ospreys and peregrine falcons, for it seemed only logical that the street names would be accurate. In truth, the weather was the only thing I didn't like about Washington State. Living in the far northwest corner of the state meant I was effectively living in rainy England.

As we sank deeper into our second winter, I became increasingly depressed, knowing weeks of gray skies lay before me. Locals, so used to dark, cloudy weather, would look up at a light-gray day and call it sunny. No wonder Starbucks started in Washington State! Drinking copious amounts of coffee was an absolute necessity, and drive-through coffee shacks were smartly placed at main intersections *everywhere* to keep us residents from returning home and curling back up into bed. Perhaps that is why Washington State is so liberal. With all the rain, intellectuals have plenty of time to read, listen to National Public Radio, peruse the aisles of their organic food stores, and spend afternoons in well-stocked independent bookstores reading about communism, environmentalism, community activism, and all the other important "isms."

Over the years, I've realized that no place is perfect and, despite the weather, I was determined to set down roots in Washington's wet, fertile soil. I had optimistically introduced myself to every neighbor who strolled by the house and through sheer chattiness on my part now had a decent circle of friends. I should have known that would spell the end. You see, I had started to feel comfortable, had gotten to know the shortcuts down back streets, and had even started to memorize where specific food items were in the grocery store when Kam announced one evening after dinner that he was being transferred. "So, Dagny, what do you think about moving to Texas?"

"Texas! You're not serious! Texas?" I clenched my eyebrows tightly, suddenly feeling a throbbing headache coming on. "Why would I want to go to Texas, of all places?" The only Texas images that rushed to my mind were of tumbleweed; dry, barren landscapes; gun-toting rednecks; and alligator wrestling. Of course, I had to remind myself, one shouldn't really judge a place until one has been there. I mean, some Americans think every Canadian plays hockey, that many of us live in igloos, and that skiing is something we can do year round. Before weather apps became popular, Americans would occasionally arrive at the Canadian border with skis strapped to their cars, thinking snow was on the ground in July. Traveling into the forests north of the border, they would eventually turn back with their skis still strapped to the roof, discouraged by a hot, humid summer, our giant bloodsucking mosquitos, and swarms of blackflies.

Interrupting my stream of consciousness, Kam continued, "The company wants me to run an office in Texas just north of Houston." Kam was eyeing me carefully, trying to gauge what level of freak-out he should expect. Then he added cautiously, "It's a great opportunity, and it's really, really sunny in Texas!"

"But that means I'll have to leave Mom and Earl, and goodness gracious, how on earth am I going to get Merlot to Texas?"

My only, strange consolation was that at least I didn't have to worry about Bear anymore. Sadly, our sweet dog had passed away a month earlier. I had sobbed through the heart-wrenching task of packing up the dog bowls that I had so lovingly cleaned and filled for thirteen years. And just a few days earlier, I had happened to find one of Bear's toy soccer balls under a shrub outside the house. I cried bitterly for hours afterward. In truth, I'd been crying for a month straight and felt like my heart was just beginning to stitch itself back together. I wasn't sure I was ready for a big change.

Thoroughly deflated by the news about Texas, I stood quietly staring at the floor, trying to come to terms with the wheels of motion that I believed would soon start spinning. I knew Kam never made work decisions lightly, and at least, to date, every move had seemed a step in the right direction. I completely trusted his judgment, and let's face it, although I worked part-time, I had no career to speak of. So who was I to say no? Kam, being the sensitive guy he is, was deeply moved by the sadness that seemed to overwhelm me and offered: "You know, Dagny, you and I are both riding now, and I'm really getting into horses, and land is cheap in Texas. You've always dreamed of having a horse property. Why don't we buy a small horse property in Texas? I'll get a horse too. It'll be a new adventure for both of us."

Stepping toward him, I put my arms around his neck and held him tightly for quite some time before giving him a kiss on the cheek. Finally looking up into his eyes, I said, "Hon, as long as I have you in my life, everything will be OK." With a long marriage comes understanding, and with much change, apparently, comes flexibility. And yes, a little bribery can go a long way.

It took a few days of Googling for me to feel better about the move, and I began to hope that my new state would live up to its nickname—the great state of Texas! I also made a solemn promise not to litter—"Don't mess with Texas"—or trespass on someone's property, as I'd heard Texans shoot first, ask questions later.

Tom was as surprised as I was about the news. "Well, we'll really miss you around here...but I can't say we'll miss Merlot," he added with a grin. "Don't worry, you'll get a lot of help in Texas. There are a lot of good horse people down there. When do you leave?"

"Probably in two or three months," I replied.

"Well, we'll have to make the most of the time we have and get that horse of yours to where we want him. You ready to get on board?"

"What do you mean?"

"I mean, are you ready to get on Merlot and start riding him?"

"Well, is Merlot ready?" I asked nervously.

"Yes, you can get on him. I've been working him every day, and he's ready to be backed."

"What do you mean, backed?"

"Oh, that means get on him for the first time. You said you wanted to be the first one on him, remember?"

"I did?" I said tentatively.

"I'll go get him," said Tom, casually leaving me.

Seriously? I thought. *Oh no, right now?* It all seemed so sudden. I felt like an actor who, having completely forgot her lines, was being pushed to the front of a theater stage as the curtain opened. I looked around nervously, trying to think up some reasonable excuse for delay when Tom showed up, tack in hand, leading Merlot into the arena. After he saddled and bridled the horse for me, I noticed how tightly Tom did up the girth. *Maybe he expects the horse to start bucking?* I worried. "Now," he instructed, "get on this step stool, and I want you to jump up. But just lean on him with your stomach—don't throw your leg over yet...no, don't put your feet in the stirrup. Just jump on his back with your belly."

I wasn't quite sure exactly what Tom meant, but I jumped up and landed like a sack of potatoes across Merlot's back.

My head was looking down on the ground on one side of the horse, and, most embarrassingly, my butt cheeks were facing Tom on the other side while my feet dangled in the air.

"Well," said Tom, "I didn't mean for you to go over that far. Get back down."

I very ungraciously slid back down as my pants went up my crotch. Merlot, to my surprise, didn't budge. "Now, try that again, but this time, don't jump quite so high. Just sort of try to get some weight on him, but keep your body on an angle, like you're trying to pull yourself out of a swimming pool and leaning on the pool's edge...OK, that's a little better. Now, try it again, but this time, put one foot in the stirrup. You're just trying to get him used to feeling your weight. OK, now get on him the usual way and throw your leg over slowly."

I felt a little more confident this time, as Tom had moved around to the front of the horse and was holding Merlot's head by the bridle. I mounted up and sat quietly, and Merlot did not budge. I praised Merlot, petted his neck, and was actually quite delighted at how quiet he was. "Tom, I can't believe I'm actually on him!" I said with a big smile.

"OK, I'll lead him, and we'll just walk."

"Sounds good to me!" I said with a laugh.

Merlot still didn't budge.

"C'mon, Merlot," Tom said, gently pulling the reins a bit to encourage him. Merlot still didn't budge. He didn't want to move. "C'mon Merlot, you can do it," said Tom, giving him another, more insistent, tug on the reins.

Merlot took one step with his right leg but then quickly moved his left leg out to better balance himself. Like a foal getting up for the first time, he wasn't quite sure how to handle my weight, and his front legs started to slide out sideways as if he was doing the splits. I realized his front end was starting to sink lower toward the ground, and I started to get worried, but then, acting like it was a herculean effort on his part, he swung his left leg out like Frankenstein and then followed with another stiff step with his right leg, gathering himself together. "Geez Louise, Merlot, I'm not that heavy. You're about nine hundred pounds, and I'm only a hundred and twenty-five!"

By now, Tom was just laughing out loud while Merlot took Frankenstein-like steps forward. It took about fifteen minutes of practice walking before Merlot realized he could walk normally *and* carry me at the same time. "OK," Tom said. "He's doing great now. Give him a little praise, and we'll end it there."

"Well, that was kind of short, Tom. Shouldn't we practice more?" I asked, puzzled.

"No. With horses, you always want to end each lesson on a good note. It's really important that you quit when the horse is doing something right. That way, he remembers the ride as something positive."

I got off Merlot, and looking at Tom with a smile, I added, "You know, Tom, I think it's good for us humans to end on a positive note too!"

For the next few weeks, we worked Merlot under saddle in the round pen, eventually getting him to walk, trot, and canter with me on him. Tom's training was a godsend, and the horse was doing better than I expected. Tom did warn me, though: "Remember, Dagny, we are doing all this in an environment he knows well. You're going to have to put a lot of miles on this horse before he'll be calm outside of this enclosed area."

"Tom, truly, I think the only reason both Merlot and I are calm in the arena is because you are here! What am I going to do without you?"

"Aw," Tom said with a smile. "Don't worry, you'll be fine. Oh, and next week we'll practice trailer loading."

"Trailer loading?"

"Yeah. You do want to get your horse to Texas, don't you?"

"Yes, I guess I do."

Over the next few days, like sending a child to a corner, Tom locked Merlot in the horse trailer with another horse. He would sometimes leave them in the trailer for a few hours, and at other times, leave him in it on his own. Merlot tried every form of escape possible—from squealing to kicking to pawing—but tough love is tough love. Tom would even load him up, take him on short drives, load and unload the horse in different locations, and drive him back to the barn. Once Tom was pretty confident the horse would load safely, he wanted me to practice loading Merlot. "Now," Tom said quite seriously, "as you load this horse into the trailer, under no circumstances should you look back at the horse. Walk into that trailer like you own it, like you are sure the horse is going to get in there."

"OK, Tom, I promise."

Having loaded horses into trailers before, I was fairly confident, and lining Merlot up straight with the ramp, I proceeded to walk in, being careful not to look back. I could hear Merlot stepping onto the ramp, and all seemed well until I heard a loud thump. I could feel the horse was no longer following, so I cheated and quickly glanced back with the corner of my right eye. To my complete surprise, Merlot had slipped while walking up the ramp, fallen onto his knees, and looked like he was praying at an altar. Rather than jumping back up onto his feet, Merlot was quite perplexed by his fall and, still on his front knees with his rump in the air, was sniffing the ramp.

After a good couple of minutes, Merlot finally decided to get back up and, once standing, shook himself like a dog after a bath. Tom was bowled over, cracking up laughing. I just shook my head, looking at Merlot. "And you're the horse I'm supposed to get clear across the country?"

13

A Bag Full of Hope

The heat, already oppressively hot and humid, was causing the suntan lotion on my face to seep into my eyes. I took the bandana from around my neck and after carefully wiping my eyebrows, tied it around my forehead. Sweat was gently gliding down my back and my rubber boots were uncomfortably hot, but I wasn't going to walk back to the house just yet. Two red bridle hooks still had to be mounted onto the wall. The tack room was paneled with solid wood, and it was taking all my strength to get the screws into the wall. Making quarter turns of the screwdriver while pushing at the same time, I drove the screws into the Xs I had carefully marked. After mounting the shiny, new hooks, I stepped back and just stared at them, grinning from ear to ear—*it had actually come true.*

I remembered I was ten years old when my mother first noticed a plain, brown paper bag perched on a shelf in my room. "What's that, Dagny?" she had asked.

"It's for the future," I'd replied.

"Oh, and what's in your future?" she inquired with a smile.

"Well," I said, reaching up to the shelf to pull the bag down and placing it proudly in my lap. "I've been saving my allowance, and I went to Canadian Tire the other day and bought these." With a big grin, I motioned to Mom to come look, and with me holding the paper bag open, she peered inside.

"What are they?" she asked.

"Hooks!" I replied happily.

"What do you need those for?"

"I bought these hooks because one day I'm going to have my own barn, and I'll need hooks to put my bridles on."

"Well," Mom had said, nodding her approval, "In life, it's always good to have a plan."

I then carefully rolled the bag closed and gently put it back on the shelf. It was a paper bag full of hope.

Like many of childhood's precious things, that paper bag and the hooks inside it were lost, probably in one of our many moves from one house to another. The intention, however, mysteriously remained in a suspended state, and over thirty years later and thousands of miles away from Quebec, in, of all places, the great state of Texas, I was mounting bridle hooks in my very own barn! Perhaps the power of intention is stronger than one thinks? *Note to self: avoid bad intentions—possibility of manifestation.*

After admiring the bridle hooks for much longer than a sane person should, I put my tools away, placed an overturned bucket just outside the tack room door, and sat for a moment's rest. Pulling the gloves off my hands, I leaned my back against the barn siding and closed my eyes. From the looks and sound of it, I was now living in a tropical jungle.

Yes, Texas was a complete surprise. In fact, I had yet to see any tumbleweed billowing across a road. And instead of the dry, rocky landscape I had expected, the area just north of Houston was a humid sea of enormously tall, green trees that seemed determined to hug every roadway. Large, white magnolia trees added dramatic flair to this green background, while pink-and-red-flowering crepe myrtles, planted, it seemed, on every street corner, added color to the scene. As it turned out, my Texas yard was a beehive of activity and had nothing in common with the eerie silence and haunting whistle of a Clint Eastwood movie. Squirrels ran speedily up and down trees while white cattle egrets moved gracefully through the pasture grass. Killdeers darted constantly to and fro, luring me away from their nests with their pretended injuries. Birds of every variety sang and chattered while giant flies, crickets, and cicadas seemed determined to fill the hot, hazy afternoons with the sound of buzzing.

After listening to this symphony of nature for a few moments, I opened my eyes and watched a large, yellow butterfly waft erratically through the air. Suddenly, I had the feeling I was being watched. Looking carefully into the stand of trees to the right of the barn, I realized that two small kittens, one solid black and one dusky gray, were eyeing me from the underbrush. *They must be from the neighbors' homes,* I thought. Calling them by their official names—"Kiitteees!"—I extended a friendly welcome, but they scattered into the woods.

Unfortunately, our new property also came with more menacing inhabitants. Walking along the back of our little acreage, I had already come across a sizable five-foot snake. In truth, I don't think I would have noticed the snake if I hadn't been on the lookout for fire ants. The real estate agent had warned me about these small but fearsome creatures. When we were first walking the property together, she suddenly pulled me away from a mound I was standing on. Luckily, the ants had not yet swarmed my leg, but just a few stings by the reddish-brown devils convinced me that rubber boots should be worn at all times. To add more excitement, shortly after moving in, the friendly cashiers at the feed store had recommended I get a big dog to chase armadillos at night and a cat to kill the scorpions and moles around the house. It was a jungle out there.

Our new house—a very formal colonial with a white-columned entrance and wraparound porch—would have been quite at home on the set of *Gone with the Wind*. Except for the driveway entrance, the property was completely fenced in white vinyl and featured two one-acre parcels of grassy horse pastures, a fenced sand riding ring, and a small, aluminum-sided red barn that sat at the far end of the property. The back and sides of our parcel gave onto a lush forest of trees, lending our little hobby farm its jungle feel. Our new subdivision was "horse friendly," which meant residents were allowed to have horses on their properties and even ride around the neighborhood on horseback! Yes, the homeowner association covenants actually had it in writing: riding horses—permitted! Unfortunately, riding ATVs, golf carts, motorbikes, and scooters under twenty-five miles per hour were also permitted. Whether I would ever summon up the courage to ride Merlot past the end of our driveway was a question. I was also quite sure that at a dead run, Merlot might exceed the local speed limit.

There was no doubt that my favorite part of the property was our little red barn. It was a shed-row-style barn with a tack room and two stalls. The spacious, twelve-by-twelve-foot stalls opened to adjoining twelve-by-sixteen-foot runs. The barn floor was solid concrete and shaded by a large overhang with solid metal horse-tie posts at either end. Two industrial fans hung from the ceiling and were angled down toward the middle of each stall. These fans were wired directly into the barn's electrical system and could be turned on with light switches. When I had asked the real estate agent about them, she said, "It can be over a hundred degrees here for weeks on end, and the humidity in this part of Texas is often a hundred percent. Trust me—in the summer, your horses will plant themselves under those fans and thank you." Yes, my little barn had low-tech air conditioning. Having spent most of my childhood shivering in Quebec barns, the idea of actually trying to keep horses cool was a real novelty. I also couldn't get my mind around the idea that the stalls were open directly to the outdoors, but in Texas, airflow is more important than keeping in warmth.

After arriving in Montgomery County, I started calling Mom on a daily basis, as I was worried she would miss me. My first calls, however, were more like excited weather updates: "Mom, we've had sunshine for three days in a row! Four days now, can you believe it? OK, now five days and not a drop of rain in the forecast. Mom, the neighbors tell me we can go weeks without rain here, and we don't get any snow either! I think I've died and gone to heaven!" During my first weeks in

Texas, I spent so much time blissfully looking up at the sun that it wasn't long before I was nursing a pretty impressive sunburn.

Because of a lifetime of moving experience, I can now wield a box cutter with the skill of a samurai and was able to unpack and organize our Texas home in less than four days. This left me plenty of time to prepare for Merlot's arrival—an event I was so worried about, I suspected a gastric ulcer was coming on. With the same care and attention one prepares for a mother-in-law visit, I was determined everything would be just perfect for him. I wasn't quite sure why I was going to such lengths to please the Evil Demon. Like a parent who thinks a bigger bedroom might smooth things over with her angry teenager, perhaps I was hoping Merlot would appreciate his spotless automatic water dispenser, his large stall filled knee-deep with shavings, and the well-placed salt lick (set not too high, not too low, on the wall). And as if Merlot wasn't spoiled enough, I'd even got him a real live pony for company!

Horses, being the herd animals that they are, hate to be alone. The neighbors warned me that a horse by himself might get into a panic, start pacing incessantly, run through a fence, or become depressed and miserable. I was already nervous about the idea of looking after Merlot, never mind having to deal with him running through another fence. And heck, he was already mostly miserable. Heeding the warnings, I ran to the feed store and asked most desperately if anyone had a horse I could borrow for a month until we bought one for my husband. A few phone calls later, we found someone willing to lend me a pony.

Maybe it was Texan hospitality, but I was amazed that a complete stranger was willing to drop off her horse. We coordinated the timing so the pony arrived the same day Merlot did. Drummer was his name. He was a sizable pony, solid chestnut in color with a matching chestnut mane and tail and thick, stocky legs. He seemed gentle and calm and looked quite capable of plowing a field.

The owner explained that the horse had perfect ground manners but couldn't be ridden.

"Why not?" I asked. "Does he have hoof problems?"

"No," she said. "Anytime anyone gets on him, he immediately stands on his hind legs like a circus horse."

"Seriously?" I said with a laugh.

"Yes. We've tried every training technique in the book, and we can't get him to stop. We thought he could be a kid's lesson horse, but as you can imagine, we can't put a kid on him, and we can't sell him, so now he's just a pasture pony."

After thanking the lady for entrusting me with her horse, Drummer and I stood side by side as she drove away with her horse trailer. Looking at the pony, I could see he was happy as a lark. "Well, Drummer, you're pretty smart. That circus-horse technique is really working for you, isn't it?" I let him loose in one of the pastures, and he set to work gobbling as if it was his life's mission to help people mow their grass. I let out a big sigh. *Well, that's one horse down. One more to go!*

I had wisely decided to have Merlot shipped by professionals. Bob Hubbard Horse Transportation had been recommended, and my horse had left on his cross-country journey five days earlier. He was traveling not in the trailer's standing stall, but VIP in the box stall I had paid extra for. His route would take him from Washington State, through Oregon, and to Southern California, where he had a two-day layover before his day-and-a-half journey to Texas. The staff at Bob Hubbard patiently took all my anxious calls for updates, assuring me Merlot was doing well.

Mom had flown down to Houston to visit my new digs, and she was doing her best to distract me while we waited for Merlot's arrival. Kam had made us a wonderful dinner that night, and Mom and I were doing the dishes when we received confirmation that Merlot would arrive later than expected—not at 8:00 p.m. but at 11:00 p.m. because of traffic delays on I-10. *Goodness gracious,* I thought, *I hope he'll unload in the dark!* When the sun went down, I put Drummer in the barn and turned on all the floodlights to cast as much light as I could. I began to feel like an expectant father waiting for a very important arrival. By 10:50 p.m., I was standing dutifully by the back gate to the barn while Mom, God love her, had walked to the nearest corner and was standing under a streetlight, ready to wave the truck in the right direction. It was a dark, moonless night, and all I could hear was the sound of frogs from the pond across the street.

It was faint at first, but soon I began to hear the unmistakable sound of a giant truck. In the distance, I could see the driver stop to talk with Mom, and then he continued toward me, parking the huge eighteen-wheeler along the road adjacent to the property. The diesel brakes screeched to a halt, and I stood there stunned at the sheer size of the vehicle. *All this for my little Arabian?* I thought. The driver jumped down from the cab and said, "So, you must be Mrs. Mofid. We got all your calls!" he said with a smile. "Your horse is fine. In fact, I've been doing this for over ten years now, and I've never seen a horse eat or drink as much as your little Arabian."

"That's my horse!" I said with a laugh. "Do you mind walking him right to the barn for me?"

"Not a problem."

Two men opened the side door of the rig, and one went in and calmly unloaded Merlot. Merlot didn't give him a moment's trouble. These were real horsemen, and I'm sure Evil Demon sensed he wasn't going to get away with anything. When we reached the barn and were standing under the lights, I had hoped Merlot would be relieved to see me and maybe even show some affection toward a familiar face. Instead, he looked at me in his haughty way as if to say, "Hmm. You again?" We put him in his stall and, taking a brief moment to sniff noses with Drummer, he made one quick circle, pooped, stuffed his head into his hay, and started eating. He was in need of a good grooming, but he didn't look any worse for wear from the long journey. After I signed the required paperwork, the men closed up the truck and left with the rest of their precious equine cargo. By now, Kam had joined Mom and me at the barn, and we watched the two horses gobble their hay while moths battered the lights above us. Suddenly, a frog the size of a cereal bowl jumped onto the concrete barn floor, giving us all the heebie-jeebies. So we called it a night.

It didn't take Merlot long to realize that we, the people who delivered his food, lived in the house that he could see directly from his stall. He had arrived on a Tuesday, and by Saturday, he was already accustomed to being fed at 7:00 a.m. Like a cat who jumps on your bed in the morning or a dog that nuzzles your hand to wake you up, Kam and I were sound asleep that first Saturday when, at 7:00 a.m., we heard Merlot whinnying.

"What's that sound, hon?" I asked, half asleep and still happily curled up under the covers.

"It's Merlot. He wants his breakfast."

"You're kidding me!" I said, pulling the sheets off my head to listen carefully. There was another neigh, this time more insistent. "He's going to wake the neighbors! It's Saturday, for goodness sakes!" I jumped out of bed and ran to the window, pulling the curtain back to look at the barn. Now all I could hear was *bang, bang, bang*. There was Merlot, standing at his stall door and kicking it with his front leg. "Oh, that little brat!" I said as I started to quickly put on my barn clothes.

"Just remember, hon, that's your dream horse!" Kam said with a chuckle as he rolled onto his side for a few more winks.

After feeding the horses, I returned to our bedroom to take a shower. "You know, hon, I saw the funniest thing out there!"

"What's that?" asked Kam as he brushed his teeth.

"I saw this thin, brown-streaked bird running across the backyard, and it moved just like the Road Runner on TV!"

"It probably is a roadrunner."

"What? You mean the cartoon character is based on a real bird?" I asked, astonished.

"Yup."

"No way!" I said, laughing. "OK, I'll keep an eye out for Wile E. Coyote!"

They say you learn by doing, but with horses, you often learn by watching. During our first month together, Merlot certainly provided a good deal of prime-time entertainment.

First, we realized that the horse was a most reliable alarm clock. His morning whinnies started out softly at 7:00 a.m. sharp and then became more insistent as time passed. By 7:30 a.m., you'd better be out there with a flake of hay in hand, or Merlot would start adding more dents to his stall door.

Then there was that exciting moment one afternoon when two horseback riders rode down the street, and Merlot began galloping the perimeter of his one-acre pasture. Normally, a horse will run back and forth along the side closest to the passing horses, but for Merlot, the mere sight of these new equines was just too much for his brain to absorb, and he began running the entire perimeter of his pasture, circling at top speed like a powerful locomotive, spewing sandy dust behind him. Even passing drivers stopped to watch and wonder. Luckily, the white vinyl fencing was strong and visible enough to contain this first spasm of excitement.

Of course, the pylon-juggling act was also entertaining. So as to avoid any horse fights, I often kept Merlot in the riding ring while Drummer was in the adjacent pasture. Placed side by side as they were, it soon became obvious, even to Kam, that there was a significant difference between our horse and the guest pony. One morning, Kam was sipping coffee when he peered out the window looking toward the back of the property. "Dagny, what on earth is Merlot doing?"

"He's throwing construction pylons around the riding ring." I replied matter-of-factly, not even looking up from the morning paper. "He's been doing it for about twenty-five minutes now."

I had placed two bright-orange rubber construction pylons in the riding ring to mark two tree stumps that needed to be removed. Kam was forever driving by them on the riding lawn mower, and I didn't want him to accidentally hit the stumps. That morning, I had turned Merlot out in the riding ring, not giving any thought to the pylons. Now Merlot was running around the ring, holding a two-foot construction pylon in his mouth like a proud retriever with a stick. Occasionally, he would stop and throw the pylon high into the air like a juggler in a circus, start bucking as it flew high above his head, and then stomp it with glee as it landed. He would then grab it in his teeth, shake it like a rag doll, and take off running in circles, holding the pylon as high as he could in the air. To the right of this scene was Drummer, quietly eating away and only lifting his head occasionally to glance at the morning's entertainment.

And how can I ever forget the attempted murder? Yes, one afternoon, I happened to be looking out our bedroom window toward the pastures when I noticed a large Labrador dog wandering into Merlot's pasture. The horse seemed oddly calm, considering the intrusion, and I wondered if perhaps Merlot liked this particular dog. Unfortunately, I soon realized this was all a Machiavellian plot on Merlot's part. Once the gullible dog got close enough to him, Merlot charged it like a mad rhino, trying to assassinate it. Luckily, the dog was also nimble and fast and narrowly escaped being stomped by diving under a fence rail. I later discovered the problem: Merlot was a cat person. Yes, the barn kitties could walk between his legs and bat his tail with their paws and even play in his grain bucket while he ate. Apparently, in Merlot's mind, cats were sensible creatures worthy of his respect, while dogs were a lowly species to be wiped off the face of the planet. I ended up having to put a Dogs Beware of Horse sign on the fence. To ensure all the neighborhood dogs understood the seriousness of my warning, beside the sign I drew a large dog paw and added a skull and cross bones over it.

Unfortunately, my relationship with Merlot hadn't changed one iota since our move to Texas. Like in a Western movie, he and I were still at a true standoff, with pistols cocked. He didn't trust me, and I didn't trust him.

Trust is a funny thing in life. It can be as durable as a stone, last for decades, and be reinforced by dependability and promises met, or it can be weak as a bubble, disappear into thin air, and be virtually impossible to find. I daresay in my defense that I was the rock of dependability, while Merlot's reactions to things were unexpected, irrational, and always varying. For example, one morning as I was leading him to the pasture, without a bit of warning, rather than walk through a large yet very shallow puddle, Merlot decided to perform an Olympian-style long jump over it, yanking me off my feet in the process.

And then there was that unusually quiet evening when he spooked at a raven's caw and almost trampled me.

Of course, I will never forget the hanging. For quite some time, I had been trying to get Merlot accustomed to me touching his ears. Every time my hand got near his ears, he would tense up, raise his head, and pull on his lead to get away from me. I had read that the way to cure this fear was to just keep your hand gently touching a horse's ears even when it pulls back so that it realizes you aren't going to take your hand away and that you have no intention to hurt it. In theory, the horse should eventually relax and let you touch its ears. Of course, there is theory, and then there is Merlot.

One day during grooming, I decided to try this technique and tied Merlot to the metal fence post. The post was made of solid steel and set into the concrete floor of the barn, so I knew it wouldn't give way. While talking to Merlot in a soothing tone of voice, I gently petted his cheeks and then slowly slid my hand up his head toward his left ear. Merlot started to pull back as expected, but I kept my hand at his ear, rising on tiptoe as I tried to stay with him. This set him into full panic. He pulled back hard with his head and neck, but the pipe he was attached to was dead solid. Suddenly, Merlot's back feet slipped on the concrete floor and buckled under him. His body fell to the ground, but his halter was too strong to break, and as he was solidly tied to the post, his head ended up hanging in midair while his legs were out to the side and he flailed away desperately like an upturned beetle.

Instinctively, I jumped back to avoid his hooves and stood there panicked, my hands covering my mouth and nose, repeating the words, "Oh, shit, shit, shit." I was alone on the property and had no Tom to call for help. The nearest neighbor was a good football field away, and I wasn't even sure they were home. I began to realize I had to cut the rope or he might just strangle himself, but how was I going to even safely get near him, with those hooves kicking in every direction? Just as I was about to run to the house in search of a knife, Merlot in all his scrambling managed to overcome gravity and righted himself. He stood there looking a little dazed, like even he wasn't sure what had just happened. I waited until he calmed down and then approached him. It took me fifteen minutes to untie the now supertight knot he had made in the lead rope. I shook my head and just stared at him. "You crazy horse, you nearly strangled yourself because you don't like me touching your ears! Do you have a screw loose in that brain of yours? And I'm supposed to trust you!" Merlot looked back at me, equally upset, as if even he wasn't happy with himself at that moment.

A week later, when the farrier came to trim Merlot's feet, I was careful to warn him about the possibility of suicide by hanging.

The farrier laughed, and we decided rather than tying the horse to the post, I would hold the lead while he worked on Merlot's hooves. The farrier's name was Craig, and he arrived with an apprentice named Mitch. They were both super friendly and extended a hearty, "Well, welcome to Texas!" when they found out I had just moved in. "Where you from?" Craig asked.

"Canada originally, but I just moved here from Washington State."

"Ca-na-da? So, I guess you say 'eh' a lot?" said Craig with a smile as he bent down to start working on Merlot's feet.

"Yes, I do." And after a bit of silence, I added, "So, how long have you've been a farrier?" I wanted to get a better sense of the man's experience—after all, I really knew nothing about him.

Craig looked over at Mitch and asked, "How long has it been now, Mitch? Two months?"

"No, boss, I think it's three now," Mitch replied with a smile, and I could tell they were teasing me.

"Don't worry, ma'am," Mitch said. "Craig didn't learn this from the back of a pickup truck. He went to farrier school."

Merlot stood quietly and dutifully picked up his feet for Craig. Like a child who is always well behaved at a friend's house, Merlot was good as gold with everyone but me. After finishing Merlot's hind foot, Craig straightened up gingerly, holding his back with his right hand and obviously in a bit of pain. "Truthfully, I'm getting too old for this. I guess that's proof I've been doing this for too long," said Craig, but he continued working on Merlot's other feet. When Craig was done with the trimming, Mitch took over and rasped the hooves smooth.

Earlier that day, I had placed some cat food near the forest, trying to entice the kittens I had seen to eat. One of the kittens, the solid black one, had tentatively come out to gobble my goodwill offering. While Mitch worked, Craig noticed the kitten and said to Mitch, "Well, look there, Mitch. That there's some nice fish bait, ain't it?"

Looking up from his work, Mitch glanced toward the kitten and replied, "Looks good to me, boss."

"What?" I asked, perplexed.

"Don't you know, Miss Dagny? In Texas, we use kittens as fish bait." Craig said matter-of-factly.

"You're not serious," I said, my brow scowling into a *V*.

"Yes, the bass really like them, and the catfish too, right, Mitch?" Craig said, looking toward his partner.

I was about to protest the horrible practice when the two of them burst into laughter.

"Aw, we're just messing with you! We don't use kittens as fish bait!" laughed Mitch.

I said, "Well, that's good to hear!" and then added, "Craig, do you know anyone who gives riding lessons, or do you give lessons? I need of bit of help with my horse."

"No, I don't give lessons," Craig replied. "I'm pretty handy with a horse, and people are always asking me to give them lessons, but in truth, it's easier to train a horse than to train people, and I don't always give people the advice they want to hear."

"What do you mean?" I asked, curious.

"Well, just the other day, this lady calls me up. I've been trimming her horses, and she's new to the area like you are, so she doesn't know a lot of people. Well, she calls me up on her cell phone all in a panic. She was trail riding, and her horse dumped her and set off running down Honea Egypt Road, which is a busy street. So she asks me what she should do."

"Well, what did you tell her?" I asked.

"I told her to start running the other way before someone finds out it's her horse!"

"Oh my gosh, Craig, you didn't say that! Are you pulling my leg again?" I said, laughing.

"No, I'm telling the truth. But then I told her not to worry: 'This is Texas, and someone will catch your horse for you.' Sure enough, a cowhand roped her horse and walked it back to her."

Before I knew it, Craig and Mitch had finished up. I walked with them back up to their heavy-duty Ford truck that was parked in the driveway, and they got in. I piped up, "Oh, before I forget—I'm looking for a calm horse for my husband, a beginner's horse. Do you know of any for sale?"

Craig answered, "I have a few young'uns for sale, but none of them would be good for a beginner. But I do know a fella who specializes in beginner horses." He found a piece of paper in his truck console and, finding the man's name and number in a leather address book, he wrote it down. Handing the paper to me through the truck window, he said with confidence, "This guy will get y'all a good horse."

"Thanks so much!" I said and waved good-bye as they backed their truck up the long driveway. I had met my first real Texans, and it turned out they were as nice as could be!

Returning to the barn, Merlot was miffed I had put him back in his stall rather than the pasture. As I opened his stall door, he pinned his ears at me. I looked at him and said, "I swear to God, Merlot, you bite me and I'm going to clobber you!" To put him in a better frame of mind, I led the Evil Demon onto the grass, disengaged his hip in both directions (i.e., made him go in circles), and then made him back up for a good thirty feet. These were all techniques Tom had taught me. When I finally let Merlot stop, he let out a big sigh as if to say, "Fine! Have it your way!" He then walked politely by my side to the pasture.

I daydreamed about the possibility of finding a truly good horse for Kam. I had already decided the horse had to be a gelding, older than fifteen, calm as a cucumber, and definitely not argumentative! He needed a horse that had been there, done that, and got the T-shirt. And it didn't matter if the horse was ugly as sin. As is true with people, good looks aren't always what they're cracked up to be, and real gems sometimes have swaybacks and knobby knees.

14

Commander of the Armies of the North

We named him Maximus. Whether he would live up to his namesake—Maximus Decimus Meridius, commander of the armies of the north, we did not know. At the time, our new horse was a very underweight sixteen-year-old Appendix (which means half Thoroughbred and half American Quarter Horse). Approximately 15.2 hands high, Maximus is solid brown with a white star on his forehead and a white snip on his nose. When we bought him, his skin was dry and flaky, and large spur scars on each side of his belly spoke a history of abuse. Given his calm demeanor, it seemed he had experienced life but had not been broken by it. Sadly, the horse had lost much of his muscle tone and his spine and hips protruded, yet his frame still had the faint echo of a former racehorse.

To be sure, his gaits were nothing to write home about. Despite his long legs, he walked like a turtle and his trot was rather choppy, but his canter was easy to sit, like a slow-moving rocking chair. I never tested him at the gallop, as I was worried he might remember his racing youth and obediently go into overdrive. The seller, who specialized in finding calm horses for beginners, had bought the horse at an auction in Louisiana just a few months earlier. Maximus had been raced, and he had the lip tattoo to prove it. And a college girl had ridden barrels on him, but the seller knew nothing more about the horse's history. Trail-testing him for over two months, the seller said that he hadn't come across anything that had fazed this horse—he could be ridden along city streets and neither ATVs nor even eighteen-wheelers seemed to bother him. The horse would willingly cross streams and step over logs; he could be ridden alone or in a group of other horses. He had perfect ground manners and was good with kids. Yes, this was what horse people refer to as a "babysitter." For a mere $1100, which included free delivery of the horse to our property and a halter thrown in for good measure, he was ours. At that price, we decided to forgo the vet check and just said a little prayer that our new boy was healthy.

Like a parent with two children, one terribly naughty and one angelic, over the next few weeks, I often found myself comparing Maximus to Merlot. Now, thankfully, we had a horse that loved attention. Maximus seemed to enjoy all sorts of brushing and even allowed us to clean right inside his ears and nose. He would stand still to be bathed and didn't make any sort of fuss with the clippers. He picked his feet up politely, never slamming them to the floor as Merlot always did. If you left him tied to a pole, he would invariably cock his hind leg and doze off. The horse would go in any direction you pointed him, load and unload into horse trailers without fuss, and seemed obliging in all respects as if his motto in life was "I aim to please."

It wasn't long before Kam was madly in love with his new horse and set about feeding him the best grain and vitamin supplements money could buy. After work, he would spend hours online, searching for natural remedies to soften and shrink the horse's spur scars, strengthen his brittle hooves, and add moisture to his dry, flaky skin. Unfortunately, Maximus seemed to suffer from chronic eye infections due to flies. So in addition to purchasing three different types of fly masks for the horse, my husband concocted a healthful eye cleanser by mixing black tea with eyebright. Three times a week, Kam would soak wads of soft cotton in this homemade solution and apply it like a warm compress to Maximus's puffy eyes. Even if the tea mixture dripped down his big cheeks, the horse would stand quietly, apparently grateful for the much-needed nursing care. It took about eight months, but Maximus eventually put on weight, regained good muscle mass, developed a shiny coat, and exuded health and happiness. Now, to be fair, Merlot was equally in top physical form and had always been in perfect health—it was just the happiness part of his character that was missing.

With Drummer's departure, Maximus became Merlot's pasture mate. From day one, even though Merlot was quite a bit smaller and much younger than Maximus, Evil Demon was definitely boss horse, having made it clear to Maximus that he was willing to kick his head in if he dared challenge his authority. So, just as we all did, Maximus quickly learned to give Merlot a wide berth. As time passed, however, they did develop some camaraderie. On cooler mornings after turning them out to pasture, I would sometimes see the two horses both on their hind legs in mock battle. It was curious, but Maximus seemed to be the instigator, wanting Merlot to play with him. The fights looked vicious, but in truth, their hooves never made contact, punching the air at one another from a suitable distance. Although he would indulge Maximus in play, Merlot was not generous by nature and always hogged the tastiest patches of grass. And like a brother who sees a sibling play with a long-forgotten toy and suddenly wants it back, Merlot would see Maximus innocently drinking from the water trough and make a mad gallop clear across the pasture just to herd Maximus away from it. Like the Grinch, Merlot was greedy, and the water trough was *his, all his, for all eternity*! So, as it turned out, Maximus wasn't much of a commander and likely would have been stabbed in the heart by Merlot if he hadn't relinquished all power.

Now that he had a horse of his own to ride, Kam was eager to explore the neighborhood on horseback. Although I had been riding Merlot regularly within the confines of our solidly fenced riding ring, the thought of actually leaving my comfort zone was as appealing to me as going to the dentist. Yes, it was something I had to do, but I just didn't want to. If you think about it, you'll notice some irony to this status quo: Kam, with only twenty riding lessons under his belt, was fearlessly excited to hit the trails, while I, after years of lessons and being the owner of an Arabian (a horse genetically designed to handle the rigors of cross-country travel) was stressing over the thought of even crossing the street. In other aspects of life, I wouldn't classify myself as a naturally fearful person. Neurotic, yes; fearful, not really. And I wasn't really that scared of falling off the horse, as I certainly had had my share of tumbles over the years. My greatest fear was that somehow I would get ditched and Merlot would gallop through the neighborhood, careen into cars, run through a barbed wire fence, or commit a more disturbing act (like kill a neighbor's dog). Yes, as we knew, in Merlot's eyes, all dogs were fair game. But I also knew that if you don't face your fears, you will never conquer them. If I was to make strides in any direction, I just had to take a pitchfork, pile all the imagined disasters into a wheelbarrow, and dump them out with the rest of the manure. Easier said than done.

Strategically, I picked a quiet Sunday morning for our first ride. Convincing Kam it would be prudent to stay close to home, we agreed we would go for a short ride in the field across the street from the house. The field was an undeveloped, five-acre subdivision lot that was maintained by a rancher who also owned the adjoining cow pasture. It was partially treed and had mostly sandy soil. The terrain followed a slope that you could ride from the very top down to a retaining pond at the bottom.

After saddling the horses and carefully securing our riding helmets, we mounted up. Watching for cars from either direction, we quickly trotted across the road and onto the grassy easement on the other side of the street. Kam was perfectly relaxed, and he and Maximus were like two peas in a pod, while I on Merlot was nervous as all get-out. You have to understand—in my mind, there was a lot to be fearful of. *A car could start honking. A tree might fall unexpectedly. A pheasant might fly out of the grasses. The cows in the adjacent field might approach—or, even worse, what if they mooed? Did Merlot even know what cows were?* I tried to blot out the many dangers racing through my mind by literally staring at the passing trees, focusing on the shapes of the leaves, and even pretending to myself that I had a deep-seated interest in pinecones.

Completely oblivious to my apparently well-hidden terror, Kam set off at a trot and then a canter. Not wanting to wrestle Merlot into a walk, I let him keep pace with Maximus. Returning to a walk, Kam changed direction and we began walking down the slope rather than up it. That's when I realized that Merlot had no sense of how to balance himself and keep his weight on his hind end. Like an out-of-control child running down a sand hill, Merlot flicked his front hooves out to the side as he careened forward, his feet hardly keeping up with the weight of his body. When we reached the bottom of the hill, I stopped him, saying, "Holy crow, horse! Use your hind end, for goodness sakes!" We then practiced going up and down the hill slowly until Merlot realized that if he shifted his weight to his backside, he could slow his forward momentum on the way down. The training work up and down the hill soothed my jittered nerves and put me in a better frame of mind.

We turned back toward the house, and I was just about to label our first "trail ride" a complete success when one of Merlot's hind legs sank into a groundhog hole. Rather than simply pull his leg out and keep going, Merlot's response was to put his head down, put all his weight onto his two front legs, and kick with both back feet, lashing out at the mysterious thing that had "grabbed" his foot. I probably could have ridden the buck out, but because we were heading down a steep slope when Merlot pulled this neat trick, I lost my balance, fell over his head, and landed on the sandy ground. With tack and bridle still on, Merlot took off like a shot, leaving Maximus, Kam, and me to watch as he crossed the street, jumped a grassy ditch, and ran back into our yard. Kam, realizing I was fine, waited as I sat on the sand and caught my breath. "Well," I said, "At least now we know he will run home." As I walked back to the barn, I made a mental note to add groundhog holes to my worry list.

Over the next few days, I questioned my desire to be a trail rider—maybe it wasn't all it was cracked up to be. Maybe I could be content just riding in circles for the rest of my life? But other riders assured me that what I was going through with Merlot was all "baby stuff"—all I needed to do was get some miles under Merlot's belt. So I took stock, dug deep, and admitted I was not the girl for the job. So, what did I do, chicken that I am? I hired a real endurance rider to ride my horse around the neighborhood. Yes, I started paying a woman named Dana twenty-five dollars an hour to ride with me—as ridiculous as that sounds. Of course, I rode Maximus while she rode Merlot, so maybe it was a fair deal.

Dana was a software programmer by day and a horse trainer and endurance rider every other waking moment. She owned eight horses, rode endurance rides on weekends, and trained young horses most days from 6:00 p.m. to 11:00 p.m. She had grown up ranching on a cattle farm, had ridden in the Houston rodeo, and spent years conditioning racehorses, so there was really nothing this woman couldn't do with a horse. She was thin but strong and kept her brown hair tied back in a long braid that ran down to her waist. Although her mother was Japanese and her father American, to me, her long braid made her look like a pretty Native American woman. Lucky for me, she had the gift of gab and was willing to share her horse knowledge with whoever asked for hours on end.

The first time Dana and I set out on a ride, her on Merlot and me on Maximus, I remember thinking, *Now, this is more like it!* Maximus was just my kind of horse. He liked to mosey and never seemed in a hurry to get anywhere. You could ride him on a nice loose rein, and if you trotted or cantered, he was always willing to slow down at the slightest request. He wasn't perfectly bombproof, and he did sometimes spook at things, but his reactions were so mild, like that inner jolt you get when someone sneaks up behind you. Merlot's spooks, however, were always dramatic and typically involved a levade, a quick 180-degree spin, and a hard gallop away from whatever scared him. And as it turned out, much like me, Merlot had a very mixed bag of fears. Solid white lines on pavement terrified him, although speed bumps were acceptable to his sensibilities. The plastic red flags on mailboxes that indicate outgoing mail were somehow evil, yet passing cars and trucks were OK. Sprinklers suddenly turning on in a yard and throwing water on his back were just fine, but baby strollers held little demons and had to be avoided at all costs.

To her credit, Dana was completely unfazed by Merlot's freak-outs. In fact, neighbors would often stop their mowing to watch as she punished Evil Demon for bucking or refused to let him flee or circled him endlessly until he calmed down. Truly, I wouldn't have been surprised if Merlot deliberately fell on his back and started kicking his legs in the air like a spoiled child. During his tantrums, which seemed to burst forth on the quarter hour, Maximus and I would wait casually on the side of the road. When neighbors approached and inquired about it, as they often did, I would reply, "Yes, it is unfortunate, but my friend's horse is a bit crazy," distancing myself from all association with the spinning Arabian. Then I would add, "But this horse," leaning over to pet Maximus's neck proudly, "is good as gold!" Merlot did, however, have one redeeming quality. Riding as we were through the subdivision, we often caught the attention of dogs that ran out to bark at us as we passed by. When a dog did have the nerve to try to chase us, Dana could turn Merlot toward the dog and charge it, causing the dog to run off, tail between its legs. It was clear—these were Merlot's happiest moments.

As a trainer, Dana made use of every natural obstacle we came across. She would see a thick stand of trees with no obvious path and decide she and Merlot were going to walk through it. A field of saddle-high grass was just an opportunity to get Merlot used to things touching him. Ditches were crossed not only down and up, but also along their length at the bottom. Streams were to be forged, logs walked over, and sandy hills traversed. We began trailering Merlot to different sites, making him walk, trot, and canter forest trails, wade into lakes, and back through narrow openings. Yes, my horse was in trail-riding boot camp, and I was an amused spectator, watching from the comfort and safety of Maximus's back. When Merlot completely balked at a new endeavor, Maximus and I would often attempt the obstacle first, proving to Merlot, for example, how a large puddle is not really a dangerous hole in the earth's crust and how stepovers can actually be stepped over and don't require a running leap.

Riding Maximus, I realized that he too had a bit of character. When running side by side with Merlot, he absolutely refused to be second. The years of racehorse training had instilled in him a desire to win, and his hind end could suddenly turn into a rocket launcher, leaving me breathless and Merlot truly surprised. Although I initially enjoyed these gallops, on one occasion after we had left Merlot in our dust, we were flying down a sandy road that was thickly treed on both sides. We were at full gallop when a deer bounded out of the trees, causing Maximus to jump sideways about eight feet in one stride. I nearly ditched it but then quickly pulled up, vowing never to let Maximus motor unless I had clear, sweeping views in all directions. Yes, every single fear-inducing moment of your life makes you take stock and think about what you are doing. There are some people who enjoy these adrenaline highs and even look forward to the next wild dash. Me? I guess I'm just more prone to the fetal position.

Watching how Dana handled Merlot's every outburst with calm deliberation, I would sometimes gather up a strainer full of courage. I would then ask Kam to hook up our new horse trailer so we could enjoy a trail ride together. After battling Merlot to get in the trailer and then becoming flustered with his dangerous, mad dash out of it, by the time we saddled and mounted up at any trailhead, I was already in need of a Valium. Without fail, just as we were about to leave the trailer area, other horse people would approach and comment on Merlot's good looks. "That's a fine animal you have there," or "Wow, that's one good-looking horse!" I would smile and thank them politely, whispering to Merlot as we rode off, "If they only knew your nickname is Evil Demon and how often I think of putting you in a straitjacket!"

In endurance riding there is a saying: "To finish is to win." After a few hours of "fun" trail riding on Merlot, I was always sincerely grateful for the finish. When we got back to the trailer, Kam and I would reward the horses with pats and treats. I would then stand beside Merlot, trying to reinforce the positive. "Well, Merlot, there was that one fan palm you didn't spook at, and I must say, your freak-out when that stick got caught in your tail was not really over the top. And yes, those deer were scary, and you only ran a half mile through the underbrush this time." The drives home from our rides were always quiet affairs. Trying to hide my angst from Kam—especially knowing the expense he had gone to in order to support my "dream"—I would look out the truck window, pretending to watch the scenery but all the while wondering: *Did I just get lucky this time? What if next time, I have a serious fall or become paralyzed? Is Merlot worth the effort? Heck, every other day you hear about a horse person breaking her back or ending up with a serious head injury. Am I going to be able to train this horse to be the horse I want him to be? How many miles do I have to put on him before he settles down? Or should I just throw in the towel and admit defeat?*

One evening after a particularly harrowing ride that left me utterly frazzled, I e-mailed my old trainer, Tom from Washington State, for advice. He knew Merlot well, so I could trust his opinion. His response? "First of all, let me say that you will never be able to turn Merlot into a calm, relaxed trail horse. He was made to be an endurance horse, and he will leave the calm quarter horse in the dust, but the calm, relaxed ride will not happen." The "will not happen" part seemed rather definitive, but I guess Tom was my Dr. Phil, telling it like it is. The question was, what did I really want? But just as the winds of indecision were gathering in my mind, to my surprise, a storm was also brewing over Texas.

When we moved to Texas, I had given no thought to hurricanes. Yes, I had a faint notion of the idea of them, but for me, they were only colorful swirls on the evening news, something that happened elsewhere, down in that bottom right-hand side of the US map. When we heard Hurricane Ike was fast approaching and building speed, it suddenly hit home. *Holy crap! We live down on the right-hand side of the map!*

On September 1, 2008, Ike was only a tropical storm west of the Cape Verde islands. By September 4, it was a category four hurricane and on everyone's mind. We would have left in advance of the storm, but we didn't want to leave the horses and we really didn't have anywhere to take them. Having only recently purchased a horse trailer, we weren't even that comfortable driving it yet, never mind trying to trailer Maximus and Merlot hundreds of miles north. Some of our neighbors had been through storms before, and they put our minds at ease, saying hurricanes were never as bad as they said on TV.

"Y'all just board up your windows or take painter's tape and use it to make big *X*s on them. That reinforces the panes. Take everything that's loose around your house, like lawn chairs, and put them in your garage. Make sure you have emergency supplies, and y'all'll be fine, you'll see. We go through this every year." Their sweet calmness eventually swayed us toward our decision to ride out the storm.

I called local horse barns to seek advice on what to do with the horses during a hurricane. Some people told me to leave them to fend for themselves in the pasture, while others said to leave them in the barn. Everyone said to take their halters off in case they ended up running through the neighborhood, "as you don't want them to get hooked on a tree branch." I noticed many horse people had spray-painted their phone numbers on their horses in case they got loose. I admit this was a good idea, but I was sure Merlot would have had a complete meltdown if I'd approached him with a hissing can of paint, so I went to Staples and made plastic-laminated labels with my phone number on them. The labels were cut like ribbons. On the afternoon of September 13, the fateful day Ike was to hit Galveston, I put the horses in the barn, took their halters off, and wrapped the labels around their ankles. As I bent down and carefully made sure the labels were on securely, I couldn't help thinking, *Boy, I never thought I'd be doing this!* Standing up again, I took a step back to look at my handiwork. The horses looked like they had just been admitted to hospital, their ID tags effectively wrapped around their wrists.

Kam came home early from work that day, as did most everybody in town, and we fed the horses and placed extra buckets of water in their stalls. We also filled a giant water trough with three days' worth of backup water for the horses. I was so grateful for the days of warning that technology and humanity's ingenuity had given us, because looking up at the sky that afternoon, we saw not even a hint of a storm.

Once the horses were looked after, we walked back to the house, ready to batten down the hatches for the night. I promised myself that no matter what happened, I wouldn't risk my life to save the darn horses. I would stay in the house. One of the feral kittens I had befriended, the black one, was milling about, so I coaxed him into the garage with food and locked him up for the night. With everything that might fly around outdoors, it was surely better for the cat to be inside. Watching the news until about 11:00 p.m., we went to bed anxiously awaiting what was now said to be an epic storm clocking in with 145-mile-per-hour winds. By 2:00 a.m., the noise of the winds was so horrific, Kam and I put blankets on the floor of our walk-in pantry, and we huddled down with a flashlight and emergency radio at our side. The pantry was in the middle of the house, the only room without windows, so it seemed the safest place to be.

The sound of a hurricane is something you never forget. Like an angry God, it is a force you cannot reckon with. Rain, wind, sticks, and tree branches battered the house, and I was convinced a window or even a wall might give way. Suddenly, around 4:00 a.m., just as the eye of the storm was overhead, we heard a huge crash, and both horses screamed.

"Oh my God!" I cried. Kam opened the door of the pantry and ran to a window to try to look toward the barn. "Whatever you do, don't go out there!" I yelled.

"I can barely see the barn, but I think it's still standing!" cried Kam as he ran back to me and the safety of the pantry. The ferocious winds lasted two more hours and gradually died down to tropical-storm strength. Realizing the worst was over, we fell fast asleep on the pantry floor, thinking there wasn't much we could do until morning anyway.

Opening the pantry door the following morning, we were greeted by a beautiful, sunny day. There was not even an echo of the night's devastation in that brilliant blue sky, but the yard was a different story. After letting the cat out, I ran to the barn and was thankfully relieved both horses were unscathed and looked no worse for wear. The largest tree on our property had come down in one of the horse pastures. To give you a sense of the size, the upturned roots of this stately tree were a good eight feet in diameter. It was the crash of the tree that had likely scared the horses and made them cry out in fear. I was so grateful I had made the decision to leave them in the barn. If I had left them in the pasture, that tree might have crushed them.

Our house had lost some shingles, and the yard and pastures were a mess of downed trees and branches, but we thanked God for our good fortune. Others weren't so fortunate. Many bigger, older trees had crashed into neighbors' houses, and on one street, all vegetation had been completely obliterated. Soon a story circulated about a family in Conroe that had had a tree with a large wasp's nest crash into their house. As if to add insult to injury, not only did the tree destroy their kitchen, the wasps chased the occupants, stinging them mercilessly.

Kam spent the next few days first purchasing a generator and then driving around with neighbors trying to find gas to keep it running. We hadn't realized that gas stations without power can't pump gas, and long lines had formed at the few that were still operational. The men of the neighborhood pulled together, helping each other connect generators and sharing tools and advice. Texans are such a friendly lot—the storm actually became a nice opportunity to meet the neighbors. Craig the farrier even dropped by in his truck to check on us. He and his ten-year-old son, Colt, had been busy clearing trees from their neighbors' yards. "Golly," said Craig, "many of my neighbors have lived on our street forever. And when you see your eighty-year-old neighbor trying to drag a big branch down his driveway, you can't just drive by. And I'm real proud of my boy here," said Craig as he glanced at Colt in the passenger seat. "Why, he worked alongside me all day yesterday, clearing brush and chopping trees. We worked nine hours straight, and this boy never complained once! Anyway, y'all just give me a holler if you need anything!" he added as he pulled away.

Since homes and businesses didn't have power, families had nothing else to do but clean their yards. Soon enough, the streets of our subdivision looked like paths through a lumber mill as everyone piled branches and logs at the edges of their properties. When the power was finally restored six days later, we watched media coverage of Hurricane Ike for the first time and understood the immensity of the storm and the serious damage it had caused in places like Galveston. After seeing the footage, Kam and I vowed that the next time a hurricane rolled in, we would roll out with the horses.

Life, though, is fickle, and one never knows what is around the corner. As it turned out, the next time I found myself rolling on wheels, it was in a wheelchair and into the emergency room.

15

An Ornamental Disaster

One doesn't expect to be hurt by a Christmas tree. These stately, green pyramids, always so still and quiet, seem uniquely designed to fill our lives with the sweet smell of pine and a good dose of nostalgia. Yes, it is true, if left without sufficient water and rubbed on by faulty wires, they can burst into flames and destroy your home. And, of course, they have been known to topple when pounced upon by a family cat. But in most cases, they innocently spend the holiday season standing in a corner, casting soft, twinkled light around one's living room. And except for the equine-themed Christmas card that shows a dapper little horse carting a felled fir home to the hearth, one doesn't really associate horses with Christmas trees. So when I found myself explaining to the emergency room nurse that my horse had spooked at a Christmas tree and thrown me, her laughing eyes and lifted eyebrows invited me to continue the story.

To understand the story, however, one must understand horses. According to my research (which I had plenty of time to do during recovery), it seems that when horses travel a specific path, they take mental pictures of their surroundings, and the placement of objects within those surroundings is important to them. In nature, horses are prey animals, and the ability to watch for potential predators and to pay keen attention to their surroundings was, at some point, key to their survival. Perhaps this is also why horses have a superb sense of direction. I had noticed Maximus's excellent sense of direction on the trails. Indeed, he has a 100 percent accuracy rate for choosing the correct fork in any road, dependably bringing us back to wherever we park our horse trailer. When riding a new trail, I've even tried to trick him on our way back, steering him in the wrong direction. Maximus will look in the direction I ask him to go but actually walk in the direction of the trailer as if to say, "I politely disagree. The trailer is *this* way."

I also read that a horse will often be surprisingly calm on a new trail because he has no expectation of what should or shouldn't be there. But if you take a horse on a trail he has traveled many times, and suddenly he comes across a new object that was never there before, a horse may, depending on its sensibilities, either shy away from the new object (a normal response) or have a major meltdown (the Merlot response).

Also, horses actually see things in different ways than humans do. We humans, being the world's most successful predators, have forward-facing eyes and can focus on and correctly identify objects up close and at considerable distances. Because of the placement of a horse's eyes, it is harder for horses to focus on objects directly in front of them and easier for them to see things that are beside them. Horses have better peripheral vision than humans and will often see objects with one eye rather than both. To give you a sense of the difference, a human can quickly identify a piece of paper floating through the air in front of him and realize it is nothing to worry about, while a horse will see that same paper in front of him as a moving, blurry shape and will likely be frightened by the movement. This is why, to better assess any danger, a horse will often turn its head to one side and try to use just one eye to focus on an object.

Horses also need to learn about things from their left and right sides. For example, if you introduce a young horse to a new object, like an orange bucket, and that orange bucket is always on the horse's left side, if you move the bucket and place it on his right side, a new location, the horse may react as if he has never seen a bucket before in his life. This is why you often have to let a horse approach an object from many angles before he really becomes accustomed to it.

As you can imagine, all these unique traits and qualities have the potential to add a good deal of excitement to any rider's life! So, the next time you see a horse walking down a parade route, just stand and salute as a compliment to its training, experience, good nature, and sound mind!

Now, getting back to our story and the day of the accident...it was New Year's Day, and I was actually feeling quite calm as Dana and I headed out for a morning ride around the neighborhood. I don't know why—perhaps I was drunk with New Year's optimism—but I boldly decided to ride Merlot and let Dana ride Maximus. *The roads will be quiet as people sleep in*, I thought, *so what could go wrong?* It was the New Year, after all. Things were going to be better this year! Even the weather seemed to concur, since that New Year's Day was ushered in with a beautiful, blue sky. Yes, the trees had lost their leaves and the lawns had already taken on a brownish hue, but the air was crisp and clean, and I was glad to be entering another blissfully bug-free winter. Indeed, I had grown to love Texas's mild winters, which, at least temperature-wise, reminded me of a fall day in Quebec.

Even the smallest lots in our subdivision were one-acre parcels, and equestrians were allowed to ride the first twenty-five feet of anyone's property. As such, Dana and I decided to ride the grassy edges of people's lawns, crossing the concrete driveways as we reached them. We had followed the very same route around the neighborhood many times. The horses seemed in good spirits and were walking calmly, so Dana and I chatted away, not expecting any trouble. About an hour or so into our ride, walking on the grassy easement of a thickly treed lot, we turned left around a blind corner. About fifty feet after we turned the corner, however, things went south—due south!

To get a head start on Monday's garbage pickup or perhaps in a fit of anger, someone had dragged their entire Christmas tree, still fully decorated, to the very edge of their driveway. The tree was covered in ornaments and streamers, and a bright, gold star hung lopsidedly from the tip. Brightly colored plastic was wrapped around the base of the tree, and Christmas tree lights poked out here and there. Maximus was a little ahead of us, blocking our view, and came to a stop to examine the tree. When Merlot walked up alongside him and finally saw the tree, I don't know whether it was his sight or mental capacity that was blurred, but he reacted as if the tree was a cannonball. In a split second, Merlot started running backward like a soccer referee—a feat not really natural to a horse. It happened so fast, I was flung forward, stopped only by his head and neck, which he was holding high in the air. Without time to gather up my reins, I clung to his neck for dear life.

After a few yards of running backward, Merlot turned sideways, keeping his left eye on the "vicious" tree. Finally, grasping the reins, I pulled back and we ended up doing a superfast side pass along the easement between the tree line and the ditch. Taking one last terrified look at all the ornaments, Merlot made the firm decision that he was outta there, and launching himself onto his haunches to spin away, he catapulted the both of us right into a stop sign! *Full stop!* I hit the red sign while he hit the metal post. Crashing to the pavement, I heard the sign swing metallically back and forth above my head and, looking up, saw Merlot running away on all cylinders.

Our house was about three miles back, but somehow, I knew my crazy Arabian would find his way. My left foot had smashed onto the pavement and was pretty beat up and swelling quickly. My hands were bloodied and studded with small pieces of gravel, and I suspected my right shoulder was bruised from whacking into the sign, but it was my left foot I was worried about. Not able to walk, I let Dana help me get on Maximus, and she led me home as if I was on a pony ride. Much like a scared child, I cried and sniffled, wiping my tears with my shirtsleeves, trying to absorb the shock of the fall while picking the gravel out of my hands. Dana did her best to cheer my spirits, and by the time I reached home, I had recovered emotionally. "Well, Dana, we always did say Merlot was a Grinch—maybe he truly doesn't like Christmas!" I said, laughing as we turned up our street. Arriving at the driveway, we saw Merlot standing in front of his stall and looking at us as if to say, "What took you so long?"

In truth, I had to admit, a fully ornamented Christmas tree across our path had been unexpected, but by comparison,

Maximus's reaction to it had seemed ever so reasonable compared to Merlot's. Yes, Maximus was apparently a wise old soul while Merlot had psychopathic tendencies and a deep-seated flight response. Perhaps that is why Arabians are natural athletes? Perhaps all that out-of-control running from both real and imagined predators built up their stamina over the centuries? Likely if Dana had been riding Merlot, she would have quickly wrestled the horse under control. It takes a certain amount of rider confidence to manage a full-throttle equine bolt. Where Dana might have reacted with "No, you are not going to get away with this," my only thought when Merlot started his slingshotlike exit was "Oh, shit!" As in all aspects of life, how you think about things and how you react to them really matters.

The next ten weeks, I was pretty much confined to the house, forced to wear a walking boot to mend my badly fractured ankle. Poor Kam had to take on all the daily horse chores while I spent the first week with my foot perched above my heart, trying to avoid a blood clot. By week two, I was crutching my way around the house and guiltily watching Kam muck stalls, feed hay, and bring the horses to and from the pasture. He was on full horse, cook, and housecleaning duty while also managing his demanding, full-time job. As if to add insult to injury, Kam also discovered an armadillo was trying to nest under our air-conditioning unit. While this might seem like a nonevent to the reader, let me assure you, an armadillo hole is not a trifling inconvenience. The nest hole is about eight inches wide and can be up to fifteen feet in length—a mini pipeline of sorts! If we didn't do something quickly, we worried the air-conditioning unit might collapse. Trying to lighten Kam's already full plate, I offered to call our local agricultural extension office to get some advice.

"Yes, ma'am, I understand. Yes, I know the holes can be really big, and they do like to nest under air-conditioning units. But don't worry—armadillos are easy to deal with. Just take your .22 and shoot it!" I just about died laughing at this official government response. First, this Texan was assuming I had a .22 and knew how to use it, and second, he was assuming I would be willing to kill the creature. It was all so very un-PETA-like. I couldn't help thinking that if we had still lived in Washington State, animal control officers probably would have trapped the thing, housed it in a no-kill shelter, and fed it dainty armadillo treats for the rest of its life.

A few days later, I was hobbling around Home Depot on crutches, just happy to be of the house, when I decided to ask a young man who worked there how to get rid of an armadillo. "Yes, ma'am, that's easy. Well, you can sick your dog on it... oh, you don't have a dog? Well, if the 'dillo's in the nest, just take a hose and fill the hole up with water. When the 'dillo comes out, just shoot it with your .22."

I said grinning, "Thanks for the advice," and crutched over to where Kam was standing in the aisle to tell him with a smile, "We're supposed to shoot it, hon! That's the Texas way!"

Kam just shook his head, chuckling, "Boy, Texas *is* another country!"

In the end, we chose a less lethal solution. Kam rigged up an electric wire and staked it about four inches off the ground, wrapping it around the air-conditioning unit. When he was sure the armadillos were out of the nest, he turned the wire on and the creatures got a nice little shock every time they wandered back and bumped their pointy noses into it. Yes, we now had little 'dillo fencing!

It is true there is certainly something about hot climates that brings nature up close and personal. I still wasn't used to seeing lizards run up the outside walls of the house, and I was sure I'd have a heart attack if I ever found one of them inside. Their tiny feet and wiggly tails always move so spastically, just seeing the creatures sends shivers up my spine. Of course, I must admit I'm not exactly known for my courage. For example, once in Washington State, we were enjoying dinner with friends when a bat somehow flew into the house. Truly, nothing adds more excitement to an elegant dinner party than a bat flying over one's dining room table. I, being the classy hostess that I am, completely abandoned my guests, running down the hall to my bedroom and not returning until the men declared the creature captured without harm and returned to the great outdoors.

Now, bats and lizards are one thing, but cockroaches are another. Truly nothing creeps me out more than the sight of a cockroach. Unfortunately, despite extreme cleanliness on my part, in Texas there seemed no way to completely obliterate them from our lives. Why, once when Kam was away on a business trip, I was innocently reading in bed when I heard an odd sound coming from the ceiling. It was a strange metallic, scraping sound. I looked up just in time to see a very large cockroach wiggle its body through the metal air-conditioning vent above my bed. The horrible, black creature fell from the ceiling and landed on the bed covers near my feet while I almost simultaneously launched myself out of bed so fast that I broke a lamp and pinched a vertebra.

Unfortunately, there were other alarming situations to face. Nothing can put the fear of God in me quite like a Texas thunderstorm. Yes, weeks and weeks of hot, humid weather just beg for thunderstorms, and on a regular basis, fierce lightning strikes crackled the summer skies. But these were not like any thunderstorms I had ever experienced. No, in Texas, every roll of thunder was an earsplitting boom that sounded very much like a World War II shelling. These flashes of doom sent down from the heavens surely meant God was displeased, and I often found myself praying for mercy in some windowless corner of the house. Over time, Kam and I also learned that at least around Houston, rain is torrential. After a mere one or two drops of warning, you better run for cover, as buckets of water will soon drench you to the core. If clouds could speak, I'm sure Texas clouds would laugh at clouds from Washington State, saying, "Now, this here is what we in the Lone Star State call rain, not that sniveling, constant drizzle you pansy clouds put out."

As I sat on the couch nursing my ankle and waiting for the throbbing to subside, I had plenty of time to think about all the unexpected twists and turns in this particular life. While family and many good friends had stayed with me throughout the journey, I did sometimes feel I was living in a movie set where the scenery was always changing. Quebec, being a predominantly French province, and Ontario, being a predominantly English province, were two very different worlds in many ways. And now we had lived in three very different corners of the States (Connecticut, Washington State, and Texas). But it's always important to look at the glass half full. Constant change can make you more resilient and help you develop practical skills. For example, in Quebec, we managed to slide through an ice storm. And by the time we left that province, I was a confident winter driver, having learned to steer through fishtails without peeing my pants and remembering never to hit the brakes when skidding on black ice. In Connecticut, we learned about Lyme disease and tick protection. Initially, I had complete meltdowns whenever I saw a tick crawling up my pants. By the end of our stint in New England, I was confidently flicking them off like mosquitos. Now, Washington State was all about addiction, but there too we learned to adapt. After suffering through sun withdrawal, we rehabbed at Starbucks and used grande Americanos to fight off depression and any suicidal tendencies.

Over time, I also came to appreciate the subtle cultural differences of these disparate locations. In Connecticut, New Englanders seemed a tad reserved, and I got the sense I might have to live in a Cape Cod or Georgian Colonial for a few decades before being completely accepted. In Washington State, we felt oddly at home among the pasty-faced liberals and tried to make conscientious choices about recycling and whether to become vegetarian, vegan, or just eat copious amounts of raw, organic cheese. Funny enough, Texans actually reminded me of Quebecers. With their strong sense of independence and pride in their state, I imagine that if you ever put independence to a referendum, a good lot just might declare themselves "Texans first." And, like the Quebec of my youth, religion and family values have a special place in Texan hearts. The area north of Houston, where we lived, is a Baptist belt. Now, a Baptist church is a modestly decorated house of worship that usually boasts a single white spire to call the faithful. In our town and in all those surrounding it, these white spires dotted the landscape with such regularity, you could confidently expect to see one every five miles. What was even more surprising to me was that, unlike Catholic churches struggling with attendance, Baptist churches were filled to the brim on Sundays and many a weeknight.

I first realized we were living in a religious enclave when I met my neighbor's boys proudly wearing their "Got Jesus?" T-shirts. Then, when dining out in Texas, we noticed that local restaurants often shouted their allegiance to Jesus by placing large crosses in their dining rooms and, in case you forgot, sometimes even in their bathrooms. After a while, Kam and I got used to waving politely as our neighbors all left for church on Sunday mornings dressed in their finery, although we did notice they sometimes looked upon us with much sadness as they drove by, as if they worried about the state of our souls. After a few minutes of guilt, we would return to sipping our coffees while relaxing on the front porch, determined to enjoy the soft morning light and let the singsong of birds be our choir.

And it is true—everything *is* big in Texas. First, the lowly car seems quite out of favor; big pickup trucks rule the road. With no shortage of land, the roads and parking spaces are equally roomy. Meal portions are enormous, and so, not surprisingly, are the people. Yes, when you land at Houston International Airport, you cannot help but think you have landed in a nation of giants. Obesity is extremely common, and all the Walmarts are well stocked with triple-X sizes. I often wonder what the little Chinese women who sew these clothes must think. I can just see them stepping back, grabbing a shirt by the shoulders, and, holding it out in front of them, saying, "This can't be right!" Except for Dallasites, I also noticed that Texans are very casual dressers, and many seem to have a fondness for track pants. I'm not sure if this attachment to elasticized waistbands stems from Texans' easygoing nature or the fact that such pants are more comfy when you have a bit of girth.

The hearts of Texans are also big. Unless you are encroaching on their private property or their right to bear arms (which could get you shot in both instances), they are the friendliest people on the planet. Texan women, in particular, are sugary sweet and will treat you like their best friend within minutes of introduction. Mind you, there were times I was a bit taken aback by all the informality. For example, while washing my hands in a roadside ladies' room, a complete stranger felt quite at ease telling me all about her yeast infection. And one afternoon while waiting for my hair to dry at a hair salon, an older woman sat down beside me and explained how much happier she was since her husband had died. But I had to admit, there is a lot about Texas that is truly endearing. I came to love their polite "Yes, ma'am." In fact, I became so accustomed to the practice that if I didn't get a "Yes, ma'am" from a young boy, I thought the child was rude. In the end, though, it was Texans' love of horses that completely won me over. After weighing all the pros and cons, I decided that any place in the world where you can drive around and see horses just about everywhere, where cowboy hats are stylish, where snazzy horse trailers take to the roads, and where you can ride outdoors in bright sunshine year round was just fine by me.

Yes, it was during those weeks of sitting and thinking that I realized I liked my new state more than I had ever expected. I also had a good deal of time to ponder the Merlot question: to have or not to have? Now, a fractured ankle is a fairly minor injury in the grand scheme of things. Dana herself had broken a leg, a wrist, an arm, a shoulder, and her pelvis in various riding accidents over the years and had never let those minor setbacks trouble her in the least. And heck, Olympic downhill skiers crumple themselves up in myriad ways, but they always seem to plough through rehab and return to the slopes. In truth, I wasn't worried about breaking a leg or arm—it was the potentially more serious accident that was cause for concern. Believe it or not, statistically speaking, horseback riding is more dangerous than motorcycle riding, skiing, football, or rugby.[1] Would I ever forgive myself if somehow, because of Merlot, I ended up with a traumatic brain injury or paralyzed? I may not be the sharpest tool in the box, but I do value basic cognitive skills and being able to move all my limbs without assistance.

A more experienced or just plain gutsy rider like Dana could handle Merlot just fine. In fact, with the right person at the helm, I was confident the horse could one day be a really great endurance horse. My Arabian needed someone who would put miles on him, ride regularly, and expose him to a lot of new situations. I had had Merlot for four years now. Although I cared about his welfare and would never want to see him mistreated, I had never really bonded with the horse. Like a couple in a bad marriage, he and I argued constantly.

---

[1] Chad G. Ball et al, "Equestrian injuries: incidence, injury patterns, and risk factors for 10 years of major traumatic injuries," presented at the 93rd Annual Meeting of the North Pacific Surgical Association, Spokane, WA, November 10–11, 2006.

He was forever swishing his tail at me, while I was forever clenching my fists at him.

After turning the question over and over in my mind, I decided we should amicably part ways. I was finally ready to shake his hoof and wish him well along any path he trotted. In truth, I think having Maximus and seeing what a really calm horse is like was a big part of the decision. Buying a horse is much like choosing a husband. You really should know whether you want to be married to a race-car driver or adrenalin junky or if you would be happier with a couch potato willing to hold your hand while you watch a movie on a Friday night. I had bought a "babysitter" horse for Kam and realized that that was what I needed! It had been stupid of me to buy a green, untrained horse and think I could get him to where he needed to be. Yes, sometimes you do learn more from your mistakes than your successes. I also think that because Merlot was my first horse, I had hung on longer than I should have, hoping he would morph into the prince I had wanted him to be. But sometimes a dream is but a shadow. Sometimes you do have to let go so you can adjust and chart a new course.

16

Saying Adieu

Life is sometimes a patchwork quilt that you try to piece together into something meaningful. And, like any good quilter knows, sometimes you just have to rip out a square if it doesn't fit. I decided to give Merlot away. I didn't want to post an ad online or put up a flyer at the feed store and sell the horse to just anyone. I wanted to give him to someone who was a good fit and an avid trail rider.

Sadly, humans are often cruel, ignorant creatures, and in the wrong hands, horses can be subjected to terrible abuse. We've all heard the horror stories: a horse fed so little it became an emaciated shell of skin and bones, a horse with hooves left to rot or left to grow so long they twisted into deformity, horses with untreated sores, or horses that went blind because of an eye infection no one looked after. If such horses are lucky, someone will take notice of their plight and take action. There is another type of neglect, however, that is less obvious. Some horses are purchased on a whim or for a child who afterward loses interest. These horses stand in stalls or pens all day, looking out from their jails with hopeful eyes, waiting for any attention. I call these horses "the forgotten ones." Horses are intelligent creatures designed to graze and move. They want to socialize and interact with other horses. When conditioned, they are capable of traveling long distances on a regular basis. To leave these magnificent animals in a stall or small pen 24-7 is much like clipping a bird's wings or placing them in cages for our pleasure. Birds are meant to fly as much as people are meant to walk. Horses are no different—their strong, muscular legs are designed for movement. I was convinced that a spirited horse like Merlot would be absolutely crushed by confinement. Truly, the last thing this horse needed was to be cooped up in a stall all day long.

After telling all my horse friends that I was looking for a good home for Merlot, it wasn't long before a friend of a friend wanted to take him. The woman's name was Karen, and she was a lifelong trail rider who wanted to replace her older horse with a more athletic one. She also wanted a horse that was smaller than her tall Tennessee Walker. My friend assured me that Karen was an extremely capable and experienced rider, rode several times a week, and would provide Merlot with the very best of homes. One afternoon, she came by our property for a test ride on Merlot in the riding ring. She really liked Merlot's size, and the two of them seemed to hit it off quite well. I agreed that she could have the horse on the condition that if it didn't work out, she would return him to me and give me the opportunity to find him a new home. I told her that Merlot had once run through an electric fence, but she assured me her little barn had horse-safe fencing.

It was a Saturday morning when we loaded both Maximus and Merlot into the horse trailer for the last time. I thought it would be better for Merlot if I brought his horse buddy along for the ride. I also packed up all of Merlot's tack, deciding to give it to Karen since all of it was a perfect fit for the horse, and I was sure I wasn't going to buy another Arabian.

Karen's barn was only a half-hour drive away from mine, so it wasn't a very long journey. She had a good five acres of pasture for two horses and the cutest little barn set not more than 150 feet from her home. When we arrived, we unloaded both horses from the trailer. A friendly, old sheepdog ran up to greet us while a cat walked around the foundation of the house, curious but keeping its distance. I warned Karen about Merlot and dogs, but she said not to worry, that her dog was horse savvy. Handing Merlot over to Karen, Kam held Maximus while I signed over the ownership and breeding paperwork. It was strange to look at Merlot's breed certificate.

I remember how excited I had been when I first held it in my hands and felt the embossed, official seal of the Arabian Horse Association between my fingers. A profound sense of sadness came over me as I signed my name to the transfer paperwork. I had, in my own way, become somewhat attached to my crazy Arabian. You can't look after an animal for four years without caring for it.

As tears welled up in my throat, I told Kam to load Maximus back in the trailer. Karen could see I was upset, and she understood that giving Merlot away had been a difficult decision. As we drove away, I turned around to look back up her driveway. Karen was holding Merlot by the lead rope. The horse was standing calmly beside her but looking at the departing trailer as if to ask, "Where on earth are you guys going with Maximus?"

Kam was behind the wheel, and he understood the tears that streamed down my face as we turned the first corner. Trying to console me, he reached over to hold my hand and said, "I think you made the right decision, hon. You'll see." It was funny, but deep down, I think I was crying more for the loss of a dream than the loss of a horse. When we arrived back home, I was worried that Maximus might whinny for Merlot or get upset that his horse buddy was gone, but to my surprise, he didn't seem bothered in the least. On the contrary, I think Maximus was quite content to have two acres of grassy pasture all to himself. After all, there was no Evil Demon to push him around or herd him away from the water trough anymore.

I waited three days before calling Karen to see how she was getting on with Merlot. I really hoped the two of them were hitting it off OK. "Hi, Karen, I just wanted to see—how are things going with Merlot?"

"Not good," she said. There was a long pause, and I could hear tears welling up in her voice.

"What's the matter?" I asked nervously.

"There's been an accident. I left Merlot out in the pasture with my other horse overnight, and he must have spooked at something. Maybe he didn't see the fence in the dark, even though I did walk the fence line with him before letting him loose. Dagny, he ran into it at full speed! He cut his throat real bad and lost a lot of blood. He's at Texas A&M, in intensive care. I don't know if he'll make it."

Shocked into silence, I didn't know what to say or what to do. I repeated, "Oh my God," several times and just told Karen how sorry I was. I told her to let me know if I could be of any help. After hanging up the phone, I burst into tears. *What have I done?* I thought. *I shouldn't have given him away!* Apart from the electric fence incident in Washington State, Merlot had never had so much as a scrape under my watch, and he was always respectful of our white vinyl fencing, not even knocking a single board down. Part of me wanted to jump into the car and drive to Texas A&M, but another part thought that if the horse died, I wanted to remember him as he had been—strong and healthy. It was strange to feel so out of control—after all, the horse wasn't technically mine anymore.

I knew Texas A&M was a top veterinarian college, so I was hopeful they could pull him through. Luckily, by some miracle—and, I'm sure, a good deal of very skilled care—Merlot survived and was allowed to return home to Karen's about a week later. When I drove up to visit, Karen's property now looked like a fairground, as she had flagged her entire fence line with brightly colored, triangular flags, hoping Merlot wouldn't run through the fence again.

Karen and I walked to her barn. She had Merlot in a stall to keep his wounds clean. I could see the horse was moving gingerly, and his chest was still quite swollen, but he was expected to make a full recovery. Karen and I talked as we petted him. The horse was more subdued than usual, obviously still in some pain. I looked into his brown eyes and said, "What were you thinking, Merlot? Trying to give yourself a tracheotomy?" God love her, Karen still wanted to keep him. She had been changing his bandages diligently and draining off any excess fluids. I admired her dedication and caring and hoped that she and Merlot would end up really bonding through the process.

You can imagine my surprise when I called a few weeks later, only to find out she had given him away. "What? You gave him away?" I asked, completely flabbergasted.

"Dagny, he ran through the fence again even though it was flagged. This time, he banged up his leg. His injury wasn't that bad, but I just couldn't take it anymore. I couldn't take it! It is just too much stress for me!" I was really upset that Karen had given the horse away without telling me, as we had agreed I would take him back if it didn't work out. There followed a very awkward long silence between us. Somehow, hearing the stress and tension in her voice and knowing what Merlot had put her through, I just couldn't bring myself to say anything critical. Karen was the first to break the silence, saying the new owner was an avid endurance rider and a vet's assistant, and the woman really wanted the horse.

When I thought about it, I couldn't really blame Karen. She had been through a lot and probably had had to shell out a good deal of money on vet bills for her "free" horse. And knowing how well Karen had flagged that property, there was now no doubt in my mind that Merlot did have a screw loose! My only hope was that the new owner was a good person who would look after him. I asked Karen for the woman's number and called her up on the phone right away. Her name was Wendi. She seemed really horse savvy, experienced, and fully aware of what she was getting into. I was so relieved. Wendi and I promised to keep in touch, and I told her I didn't want the horse ever to end up in a bad situation and that I really did care about his welfare. She understood.

About four months later, I made another follow-up call. Apparently, Wendi's daughter just loved Merlot, and all was going well. "You know," Wendi said, "When he got here, Merlot seemed angry, angry with the world. Did he ever seem that way to you?"

"Yes, that's Merlot, all right! He was like that the day I got him!" I chuckled.

"But now he has settled in and seems much happier. You know," added Wendi, "that horse has challenged me in more ways than any other horse I've owned, and I've owned a lot!" Luckily, Wendi was up to the challenge. A year later, she e-mailed me a picture of her on Merlot atop the ridge of a mountain. Wendi looked the picture of confidence and was all smiles. She and Merlot had successfully completed a twenty-five-mile endurance ride. The horse looked terrific and in peak condition. No one was happier than I to see that photo.

17

A Band of Gypsies

The crew of Mexicans hired to help with the annual tree trimming and yard cleanup had just begun their lunch break when José turned to me and asked, "I guess your horse, he must be very 'spensive, no? We all think must be very much. Maybe twenty, thirty thousand dollars?" he asked in his broken English.

"What horse?" I asked. "My horse over there?" Astonished, I looked toward Maximus, who was gobbling away in the middle of his pasture. It had never dawned on me before, but I guess, taken objectively, it was a little odd to have a four-acre horse farm seemingly dedicated to only one horse. The crew assumed that either the horse was really valuable or I was just nuts. When I explained in my broken Spanish that Maximus was *"No es caro, más viejo, sólo mil cien dólares."* (not expensive, older, only $1,100.00), I could see from their expressions that my answer had put me squarely in the "just nuts" category.

Looking for a moment at the red barn, the nicely graded sand riding ring, and Maximus, who stood surrounded by a sea of lush Bahia grass and encircled by elegant, white vinyl fencing, I saw the excess for the first time. For these Mexicans, working as day laborers and struggling to make ends meet, I was just another "rich" American who wasted her money. There was both envy and laughter in their eyes, but the men quickly went back to work, as life had taught them they were valued for their industry. The men wore ripped shirts and tattered shoes, while their sun-weathered faces and sinewy, muscled arms spoke of years of hard, physical labor. Earlier that day, they had made a point of mentioning that they always worked six days a week. It was both a point of pride and an accusation as if to say, "We bet you never worked six days a week in your life, lady." I suddenly felt terribly guilty and wanted to explain that when my husband and I had met in high school, all we had were bicycles; to swear that silver spoons had never touched our lips; and to assure them that the farm they saw before them was a little girl's dream come true and not the latest whimsy of a spoiled wife. But who was I kidding? I could barely say *"Buenos días,"* never mind cobble together meaningful-enough words to wash away that kind of guilt. And, in truth, I had never worked six days a week.

Ever since Merlot had made his rather dramatic exit from our lives, which, in hindsight, had been almost as intense as his entrance into it, I was spending more time with Maximus, often bringing him carrots or making time to pet him. That same evening before going to bed, I noticed our yard was bathed in the silvery-gray light of a full moon. It was about 10:30 p.m., and without putting on the floodlights, I walked in the moonlight out to Maximus, who stood quietly under a large oak tree. He was standing very still with one back leg cocked, which denotes relaxation like that of a human sitting comfortably in an easy chair with legs crossed. The horse didn't budge as I walked over to him, and after giving him a carrot, I hugged his thick neck and said, "Maximus, everyone was talking about you today! They think you are a valuable racehorse or maybe a great stallion! But you and I both know, the place where you are most valuable is right here," and I tapped my hand on my heart. I then stood directly in front of his chest and tucked my head right under his. At moments, he would stop supporting his head and let its full weight rest on mine. When he did this, I would giggle, and this pleased him. He understood we did this just for fun, and he seemed to enjoy the horse-human connection. Then, after spending about ten minutes whispering sweet nothings into his ears, I left the pasture and closed the gate. I couldn't help wondering if he was sad all by himself. Of course, there was life all about him. He had a loud chorus of frogs to keep him company through the night, and I could see an armadillo shuffling along the edge of the ditch by the street. A soft flutter of wings had alerted me to an owl perched in a nearby tree, but all that didn't amount to a horse buddy. No. As I stood for a moment looking back at him, there was something achingly sad about a lone horse standing under an oak on a full moon.

The next few months were quiet affairs. Indeed, I have often noticed that after life shakes you with a bit of excitement, it often lets you fall back into a soothing routine that invites rest and contemplation. I don't know what determines the amount of excitement or the amount of rest, but we were enjoying post-Merlot calm. It was during this period that Kam and I started taking Maximus with us for our morning walks around the neighborhood. I would put his halter and lead rope on, and Maximus would plod alongside us like a dog on a leash. Truly, we could easily outwalk the horse, but Maximus seemed determined to amble along, looking at us with a curious "What's the rush?" whenever we encouraged him to speed up. Eventually, we gave up trying to get him to move faster, and our morning walks became leisurely strolls with the same forward momentum of avid window shoppers. No one else in the neighborhood walked their horses, and passers-by would joke that Maximus was an awfully big German Shepherd.

As the months went by, Maximus became known and loved by all the children in the neighborhood and graciously accepted pats and kisses on his nose whenever offered. He would stand patiently whenever we stopped to chat with neighbors and wouldn't even flinch when the garbage truck rolled by. Both Kam and I rode him regularly in the riding ring and with friends on the trails. Once a month, we would trailer him over to a local horse barn and pasture him there for a week. It was truly like dropping a child off at summer camp. With barely a glance back to say good-bye, Maximus would dart toward his new pasture buddies, excited to romp and play and make friends.

During one of these "horsey getaways," I found out after the fact that someone had placed Maximus in the field directly adjacent to the main stable, which meant he could walk right up to the building. The horses that were stabled in the barn were accessible via half doors that were open on the top. Rather than just grazing away in the pasture, Maximus was so excited by this horsey "meet and greet" opportunity, he apparently began running to each stall, sticking his head completely in the upper half of the stall doors and trying to get each horse to play with him. I was told at one point that he reared up and had flailed his front hooves in the upper half of a stall opening, scaring the bejesus out of the riding students inside the barn. A riding instructor who was watching said Maximus was just having fun and there was nothing aggressive at all in his demeanor—apparently, our boy just wanted to be the life of the party.

I had to chuckle, but it seemed to me that I had come full circle. Just as my mother had dropped me off at Covey Hill so many years before, here I was dropping off our "horse child" at "horse camp." And, I had to admit, here too there was a bit of self-interest at play. You see, after having a horse property for four years, we realized that looking after horses, and even just one horse, involves an awful lot of physical labor.

Like steady metronomes, our lives now revolved around a twice-a-day feeding of hay. Other everyday tasks included mucking out the stall, filling the water trough, sweeping the barn floor, and turning the horse in and out to pasture. Every other week, we had to clean the water troughs, refill the grain bins, and stack fresh hay. Even the easier tasks, like sitting on the riding lawn mower, were time-consuming and tedious. Bahia grass grows so fast in Texas that Maximus couldn't eat it fast enough, and we spent many a weekend sitting on the riding lawn mower for hours on end, trying to keep the pastures neat and trim. Of course, the fact that I was allergic to Bahia grass, hay, and apparently every other pollinating tree in Texas didn't help. And unlike Merlot, who I had to admit was always quite fastidious, Maximus was our Pig-Pen. He loved to roll in everything, seemed happiest when he managed to cake himself in mud, and never gave a moment's thought to where he pooped, even sometimes eating and pooping at the same time.

In between his weekly baths, the horse would become so dusty that if you patted him on the back, a cloud of smoky dust would rise up into the air. In terms of grooming requirements, I was convinced that one Maximus equaled two regular horses. Indeed, Saturday mornings were often spent trying to comb the mud out of his always-tangled mane and tail. Using a metal comb, Kam would talk to Maximus as he worked the mane: "Seriously, Maximus, how do you manage to get so dirty all the time? Don't you want to look handsome in case a mare walks down the street?" The horse would stand there, eyes shining brightly, completely delighted with all the fussing over him.

This was not a particularly easy period in Kam's life. He was now a corporate executive, spending hours on planes jetting around the world. Indeed, in one year, he traveled more than 350,000 miles. Often away for weeks, he would return home exhausted, stressed, and preoccupied with work. After he slept off jet lag, I would often find Kam in the backyard, quietly grooming Maximus under the shade of the barn's overhang. The horse, like an old soul, had a strange ability to absorb Kam's worries. I know that horses are often used as therapy for disabled children, but it seems to me they have other callings as well.

One morning, I was mucking a stall when I happened to notice my very tired husband hugging Maximus's thick neck. Tears were streaming down Kam's face as Maximus stood in quiet understanding. Somehow, the simple task of brushing the horse's coat and picking his feet was just enough to put life back in perspective.

Of course, when you love deeply—whether the target is a person or an animal—you commit yourself to the pain of loss. It was the month of September, and we were enjoying a quiet Sunday. Kam had spent the afternoon mowing pastures, while I had weeded the vegetable garden. We had both showered and changed, and I was in the kitchen pouring a cup of green tea while Kam, waiting for his tea, was looking out at the pastures, admiring his handiwork. He had pulled back a curtain in the living room window and was looking toward the far back right of the property when he said, "Hey, hon, check this out. Maximus is just rolling like crazy in the pasture. I've counted twelve rolls from side to side already."

Without even looking out the window, I grabbed the cell phone and dashed out the back door of the kitchen. Pulling on the barn boots that I had left on the porch, I raced toward the pasture. Scooting my body between the bottom and middle rungs of the fence, I was at the horse's side within minutes and encouraged Maximus to get up. "Get up! Stop it! Get up, Max!" The horse obeyed and stood up for me. Grabbing his halter and lead rope off the fence gate, I put it on him and started walking and speed-dialing the vet at the same time. I could see the pain in Maximus's eyes. They were glazed, and he was looking inward, no longer paying attention to the world around him.

When I reached the emergency service of the vet's office, I was frantic. "My horse is colicking! I need a vet to come to 110 Imperial Lane right away!" I knew time was of the essence, for I remembered a story about a horse whose intestines had twisted as a result of a bad colic. After eight hours of sheer agony, the poor animal had simply died. I couldn't bear the thought of that happening to Maximus. The on-call emergency vet was there in twenty minutes, and after giving the horse a painkiller and "tubing," which involves putting oil down his stomach, the vet told us to walk the horse until he started to feel better.

By this time, Kam was totally distraught and, taking the lead rope from my hands, started walking the horse around the riding ring, looking like he'd seen death. One of my neighbors who is also a horseperson stopped by when she saw the vet's truck in our driveway. She knew that no one calls a vet out on a Sunday unless it's an emergency. Joining me at the side of the riding ring, we began to speak in hushed tones. "Brenda, I don't know what I'll do if we lose him. I mean, with Merlot gone now, I don't even want to think of it!" My voice was choking as thoughts of my old dog, Bear, came to mind. After he had passed, it was so sad to come home to an empty house—no excited, squealing barks coming from inside the house as we opened the garage door, no doggy toys to pick up. Just the thought of losing Maximus and no longer seeing him in his stall at night made my heart clench into a tight knot.

Brenda, who had been watching Kam intently, leaned toward me and whispered in my ear, "I hope Maximus makes it, because if something happens to that horse, I think Kam is going to colic." Kam, God love him, was walking and petting Maximus's neck at the same time, trying to give him all the positive energy he could. At first, the horse kept trying to stop, not wanting to move forward, but now he was walking more steadily. After about forty-five minutes of walking, I put a stethoscope against the horse's stomach and heard his gut rumbling. This was a good sign. After another hour of steady walking, Maximus once again was interested in the world around him, his ears had come forward, and the look of pain had disappeared. He even showed signs of wanting to eat, reaching down with his neck to eat grass. We were out of the woods. We had caught the colic early enough. By this time, the sun had gone down, and Brenda had gone home. Thankfully, the wrenching pain in my heart began to subside. I prepared a moist bran mash for Maximus, and after putting the horse in his stall for the night, Kam and I walked arm in arm toward the house. The pain of losing a most beloved horse would have to wait for another day.

Later in the week, the vet who had treated Maximus drove by the house. I was pulling weeds at the edge of our property alongside the road when the vet pulled over to say hello. I asked him why he thought the horse had colicked, for I hadn't changed his feed, and the horse always had water available to him. "I don't really know why, exactly," said the vet. "It's been pretty hot the last little while. Maybe he just didn't drink enough water? Or maybe he *is* a little stressed living here by himself without another horse for company."

That same evening, I broached the subject of getting a second horse with Kam, but he suggested we wait awhile. "Why should we wait?" I asked.

"Well, I didn't want to worry you, hon, in case it didn't happen, but...well...I guess I should tell you. I was just offered a really great job in California running a solar company."

"What?" I sputtered, totally shocked. He hadn't even told me he was looking for a job. A long silence followed. Finally, I spoke up. "You expect me to give up this life we built up for ourselves in Texas? Just now that I have a good circle of friends? I love Texas! Sure, the bugs aren't great, and I know you don't like the humidity here, but you've been happy here, haven't you? Haven't you?"

"Yes, I've been happy here, Dagny, but these types of career opportunities you just don't pass up. I mean, just look around you. You wouldn't have this horse property if it wasn't for me."

"Oh, that's just peachy. You giveth and taketh away!" I replied sarcastically.

"Hon, now just calm down. We're not moving to a big city like LA or San Francisco. The job is on the central coast in a place called San Luis Obispo. It's right on the ocean. You'll love it."

"No, I won't love it!" I yelled and stomped into our bedroom, slamming the door behind me.

Kam knew enough to leave me be for an hour or two. Soon the smell of food was coming under the bedroom door as Kam cooked up a storm in the kitchen, trying to appease me by making a nice dinner. When I finally came out of the bedroom and walked into the kitchen, he was pulling a roasted chicken out of the oven. Using red oven mitts, he set the pan gently on the stovetop. He was wearing a black shirt and blue jeans but had wrapped my grandmother's baby-blue apron tightly around his waist. It was a frilly apron fringed with white lace and made him look cute as a button. I could see he had roasted baby potatoes with rosemary, and in a casserole dish beside the stove were steamed green beans. They were dripping with butter. The kitchen looked like a tornado had hit it, but the table was set, and he had even placed our fancy blue napkins on the plates. When he noticed I had come out of my room, Kam stopped to look at me, waiting to see what I would say.

After a few minutes of silence between us, I finally spoke up. "You do know what California is known for, don't you?" I said as I walked toward the counter, picking up the casserole dish to place it on the table. "We've been through an ice storm and a hurricane. You're just trying to spice up my life with an earthquake now, aren't you?" He could hear the hint of a smile in my voice.

Walking up to me and without saying a word, he kissed my forehead. We were going to California.

It was a sad day the first time I drove up to our street and saw the "for sale" sign in front of my little horse property. I wanted to walk over to the sign, yank it out of the ground, and hide it in the garage before anyone noticed it. We had moved so many times, I started to feel like a military wife with a husband who yanks her to new locales at regular intervals. But if I was sad, I was partly to blame. I should have known better. I had let things go too far. I had been bewitched by the Lone Star State. You see, the house was now completely decorated in a Texas motif. It had all started innocently with the simple purchase of a "Welcome, Pardner!" entrance mat. Soon, a metal Star of Texas had adorned the tack room wall, our wine glasses became etched with horse scenes, and family photos took on an historic character, now framed in faux wood and studded leather. *Gardening in Texas* books were strewn on the coffee tables, and cowboy statues adorned the fireplace mantel. And I have to confess that, for a Canadian, I had become oddly attached to the Texas flag. The flag's crisp red, white, and blue colors now adorned our throw pillows and placemats, and I had even managed to drape a flag proudly over the dining room table. To add to this sweet tea, the radio had been set to *Country Legends* for four years. Celine Dion was now just a faded memory, replaced by the new men in my life: Johnny Cash, Willie Nelson, and George Strait. Before Kam had told me about the move to California, I had even seriously considered buying us cowboy hats and dragging him to a Texas two-step class. *I mean, really! Who wouldn't enjoy flicking cowboy boots to the sound of a country-western song?* But that was then. This was now.

Life's compass had spun 180 degrees. As the Buddhists say, the only constant in life is change. Whether we were in a house for four years or forty, we were all just passing through anyway, were we not? And with many moves under my belt, I had realized that in terms of friendship, a move away separates the wheat from the chaff. Any friendships worth keeping would remain strong and could always be nourished by calls, visits, friendly texting, and heartwarming Christmas cards. *Isn't it true*, I said to myself, *that I am still very much in contact with friends I met four moves ago?* In the end, acceptance and trying to see the positive in a situation is sometimes the only course of action. Kam and I were the best of friends, and like Willie Nelson's band of gypsies, we were going down the highway and just hoping the world would turn our way.

18

The Golden State and the Golden Horse

Maximus was excited the day the Bob Hubbard Horse Transportation truck pulled up to the end of the driveway. It was a November morning, and after giving the horse a thorough grooming to ready him for the long journey, I put his halter and lead rope on and walked him up our driveway to the very edge of the street. It was 6:00 a.m., and the air was crisp that morning. The first rays of the morning sun had just begun to dry the dew on the grass. I noticed that the last of the fall leaves still needed to be raked up, but since it was moving week, the yard chores would have to wait for the new owners of our Texas home. The horse sensed something was up, as it wasn't our usual routine to walk and stand at the edge of the driveway as if waiting for a school bus.

The Bob Hubbard crew arrived promptly as promised. When the big rig rolled to a full stop alongside our street, Maximus heard the other horses inside it and whinnied to them. His eyes began to shine brightly as he raised his nose and curled his lip, trying to get a better whiff of the horses inside. Given his personality, I wasn't worried about the long trip to California. In fact, when the driver loaded him into the truck, Maximus was so excited that he almost ran up the ramp. There was a big, black draft horse in the box stall next to him, and Maximus, social butterfly that he is, was apparently delighted to make his acquaintance. Much like a child being dropped off at an amusement park, Maximus even forgot to give me a polite parting look before the trailer doors closed. Standing beside the truck, another member of the crew handed me a clipboard with some paperwork to sign. Grabbing the pen he offered me, I signed the documents, and handing them back, I said, "This horse won't give you any trouble. I think he finds it all very amusing!"

As if in full acceptance of our seemingly nomadic lifestyle, we decided to rent a house in our new town and board the horse. The simplicity of these transient arrangements had much appeal, and who were we kidding? After our first house-hunting trip in California, it was clear we couldn't afford anything decent anyway. Yes, for about $800,000, we could buy a small house that was in dire need of repair, likely needed a new kitchen and bathroom overhaul and, on an ongoing basis, would cost oodles in property taxes and utilities. Having moved, on average, every third year for the previous fifteen, we decided to pass on the opportunity to chain ourselves to a big mortgage payment, as appealing as that would have been.

I must admit, when we landed in SLO (yes, this is what the locals call San Luis Obispo), my sense of adventure finally kicked in, and I was anxious to discover whether our new state was indeed golden. Truly, I don't think there was anyone more surprised than I was to find myself living on the central coast of California in an area northwest of Los Angeles and south of San Francisco. Having gotten used to landing at Houston International Airport, landing in SLO seemed like a charming, nostalgic step back in time. After the little plane we were on swung its wings to and fro, we eventually settled back into a horizontal position and came to a swift landing on what seemed a very short runway. The airport was so small, we descended the stairs of the plane right onto the tarmac. After retrieving our carry-ons from a cart, we then dragged them up a wide ramp into the small, concrete building that functioned as a terminal. As it turns out, the SLO airport can only handle small, regional jets, and many residents seem to like it that way, wanting to keep their little jewel of a town all to themselves.

SLO is rated one of the best places to live in the United States, and I could immediately see why. As a university town, it has a youthful vibe and is chock-full of great restaurants, environmentally conscious organic grocers, tremendous hiking opportunities, and dedicated bike lanes. To add to the charm, every Thursday night, one of the main downtown streets is completely cordoned off from all traffic to make way for an incredible farmers' market. Many local restaurants have gotten into the act and offer tasters and small meals to university students and hundreds of other loyal market-goers. In truth, SLO reminded me of many towns I'd seen in Washington State except with copious amounts of sunshine thrown into the heavenly mix. The area is simply stunning, with rolling hills and craggy peaks alternating with wide, sandy beaches and rugged cliffs that plunge into the ocean. Quaint, small towns fondly hug this section of California's coastline, and everyone pines for a house with even a glimpse of the mighty Pacific. Indeed, houses on either side of Highway 101 seem to strain over each other's shoulders hoping for a peek of blue ocean, their windows aimed due west.

After scoping out the area and surrounding cities, we decided to live in a small town called Nipomo, just a hop, skip, and a jump away from SLO. We rented a bungalow on an environmentally friendly golf course, and I started to unpack. This time, however, the unpacking was halfhearted. I decided to leave many of our boxes unopened in the garage. I mean, really...was there any good reason to put pictures up on the wall? Like a woman determined to stay single, I wanted to leave my options open. California and I were just dating. Only time would tell if our relationship developed into something meaningful.

Unlike that of Texas, the weather in our new town was unchangingly cool, mostly sunny, and seemed content to stay between sixty and seventy-five degrees Fahrenheit year round. And Julio Iglesias is right—it never seems to rain in California. In fact, at least where we were, the weather was neither windy nor rainy, nor cloudy, nor too sunny. It was moderate in all respects, and even the morning fog seemed amenable to being burnt off by 10:00 a.m.

The ocean was now but a fifteen-minute jaunt from the house. After driving along back roads that passed fields of ground crops such as lettuce, kale, and chard, we could take a short stroll through a protected marsh and, after trudging through some sand dunes, dip our toes in the cold waves of the ever-rolling Pacific. As delighted as we were with being able to see the ocean on a regular basis, the journey did seem a bit odd. I mean, where else does a marsh separate industrial-scale farms from sand dunes and the ocean? The area did have other oddities. Nipomo seemed completely bug-free, with neither flies nor mosquitos to contend with. Interesting enough, the only things that buzzed around the house on a regular basis were hummingbirds. These miracles of flight whizzed by with such frequency that I quickly filled a hummingbird feeder to entice them to stop long enough for me to actually see them. Soon enough, there were excited battles for nectar in the backyard. And yes, I have to admit—I did burn our morning toast on several occasions, distracted as I was by hummingbird dive-bombing techniques and mating rituals.

On one of our first morning walks around our new neighborhood, Kam and I noticed a small herd of about twenty-five goats cordoned off on the golf course roughs. The goats were mostly white, but some had patches of black on them while others had patches of sandy brown. They were super cute, and all of them had short horns and long, floppy ears like basset hounds. It wasn't long before we learned the goats were official members of the golf course maintenance crew. Every week, the four-foot fencing that they were kept in would be moved to a new location, and the goats, being excellent employees, would keep the golf course roughs neat and trim. I couldn't imagine a more win-win situation, and I loved seeing these adorable creatures gobble away. One afternoon, I even caught them taking a leisurely group nap. They were all lying down while a soft breeze blew their long ears to and fro. I couldn't help laughing and thinking, *Only in California!*

Yes, all in all, moving from Texas to California is like moving from one solar system to another. We had left truck-loving Texas to arrive in a land of Priuses and solar panels. We had left the Lone Star State, where the steakhouse is king, to the Golden State, a land of juice bars and organic everything. And, most importantly, we now had the privilege of buying incredibly fresh and delicious California-grown produce—at *premium* prices. Knowing that California grows so much food for the nation, I had naïvely expected rock-bottom prices, thinking, well, that prices should be lower—after all, we were living close to the source, were we not? After a while, however, I realized that the cost of living in the state had been on an upward trajectory for quite some time.

The first time we tanked up our truck, Kam just stood by the pump, grimacing and shaking his head in disbelief. When he got back into the vehicle, he looked at me and said jokingly, "Given the price of gas, hon, I think we're going to have to start riding our bikes to the grocery store."

"Hmm...maybe all those bike lanes are a real necessity!" I grinned and then added jokingly, "That's why they call it the Golden State of California. It's a reminder to bring gold with you!" Now, don't get me wrong. I really love organic produce and incredibly trendy coffee shops. Watching surfers battle ocean waves is always a treat, and who doesn't enjoy driving by tidy, rolling orchards and vineyards? The higher cost for almost everything, however, coupled with high state income taxes and heavily congested freeways, convinced me that California is not for the faint of heart or light of pocketbook.

Thankfully, Maximus arrived in California in fine form, stepping off the horse trailer like a politician on a speaking tour. He was tired, but after taking a moment to look at his surroundings, he could see there were more horses he would have to shake hooves with.

We had decided to board Maximus at a private barn about two miles down the road from where we lived. The owners of the property, Sam and Lori, are avid ropers who compete in team roping events. They own about eight horses and set aside a small number of pens on their property for horse boarders. Their house is perched on the crest of a small hill set far back from the road. The horse part of the property is directly behind the house and follows a long slope down to the very back of the property, where there is an enormous, outdoor sand arena used for roping cattle.

Because the weather is so moderate in California, there really is no need to shelter horses in a barn, and like many horse properties in the area, this property didn't have one. The horses there are housed outdoors year round in large sand pastures and in a series of pens, one adjacent to the other. The pens are large by pen standards (probably twenty by forty-eight feet), but after seeing Maximus enjoy acres of green grass in Texas, I must admit that seeing him stabled in a sand pen, however spacious, made me cringe a bit. Despite the smaller digs, however, Maximus himself seemed thoroughly content, as he was now surrounded by plenty of other equines for company. A large, buckskin quarter horse was stabled in the pen beside him. When we first put Maximus in his pen, he ran up to the buckskin, and after a few moments of excited sniffing of noses, Maximus let out a squeal and a stomp, making it clear right off the get-go that, even though they were separated by pipe fencing, Maximus was in charge. The buckskin seemed in agreement and backed away from the fence, lowered his head, and looked away, making it clear to Maximus that he was no threat and quite willing to be friends.

When I first visited Lori's place, I was quite impressed by the thick stand of eucalyptus trees running along the right side and very back of the property. I had never seen eucalyptus before. The trees are enormous, with each one at least twenty to thirty feet wide and towering a hundred to a hundred fifty feet into the air. Because of these trees, rather than smelling like a horse property, her place had a surprising fresh, clean scent much like minty mouthwash. The first couple of times I rode Maximus in the outdoor sand arena, I had to pinch myself, thinking, *Wow! Never thought I'd ride with the sweet smell of eucalyptus!*

In the evenings and on weekends, Sam and Lori often got together with friends to practice roping, and I would sometimes stand at the edge of the arena and watch them practice. In team roping, one horse-and-rider team stands on one side of the cow chute while another team stands on the other side. Once the chute is activated by a lever or button, the calf blasts out, and the two riders are on for the chase. One rider (on the header horse) ropes the horns of the calf while the other (on the heeler horse) ropes the calf's heels. The calf ends up on its side in a rather uncomfortable-looking scissor position. At first, I felt sad for the poor animals, but the calves did seem used to the routine. Once released, they would jump back up onto their feet and obediently return to the exit chute.

It was always exciting to see Lori ride. She reminded me never to judge a book by its cover. You see, Lori is a rather beautiful and petite blond woman who is also incredibly talented with a lasso. In fact, she has won many roping championships and even worked for hire on cattle ranches, helping with branding and sorting. She once told me she had never taken a riding lesson in her life—she had learned by doing. To watch her ride, you could see it was as natural to her as breathing. All her horses were well trained, calm, and businesslike. They knew their jobs, and they weren't pets. In fact, I think Lori and Sam were quite amused at how much time Kam and I spent fussing over Maximus—but childless couples do have to dote on something.

Having never lived so close to the ocean before, I was dying to ride Maximus on the beach. One weekend, Lori lent Kam her calmest horse to ride—the big buckskin—and she trailered us over to Pismo Beach. We parked in an empty parking lot beside a restaurant and mounted up. After crossing a busy street of RVs and ATVs, we followed a quiet trail that meandered through a series of sand dunes. The dunes were covered with succulents and many scented flowering plants I had never seen before. The sky that day was a brilliant blue, and the rays of the sun bounced off the white sand, adding to the brightness. The sand was deep, but Maximus was excited to be trudging through it. At the beginning of the ride, you could smell the ocean but not see it. After about a mile, we came to the end of the trail through the dunes and the entrance to the beach. As we came over the last dune, Maximus saw the ocean for the first time and came to a full stop. It was as if he said, "Oh my *God!* That is *amazing!*" Every nerve in his body became taut and excited, and his ears were pricked sharply forward, listening to the roar, as his eyes shone with excitement. Lori's two horses (the buckskin Kam was riding and the horse she was riding) had been to the beach many times, so they were less impressed with the ocean, and Maximus followed their lead.

We first walked and trotted along the sandier part of the beach. Once Maximus got used to the sounds, I moved him to the harder-packed sand, closer to the water. I had to laugh, as every time the foam of the waves approached, he side-passed the foam as if it was dangerous. The beach was very wide and, on this one stretch, trucks were allowed to drive on the sand over to an area where ATVs could take to the dunes. I asked Lori and Kam if they minded if I went ahead, and they said no, so I set off at a fast trot. I noticed that Maximus and I were keeping pace with two young men in a pickup truck just to the left of us. The truck was driving in the deeper sand while Maximus and I were on the harder-packed sand closer to the water. I broke into a canter, and the young men noticed and drove faster in the truck to keep pace with me. I looked at the driver, and with a big grin, I leaned forward and whispered in Maximus's ear, "Show them what you've got!" I asked Maximus for a gallop. He took off like a shot, leaving the truck behind, and I let him run like I had never let a horse run before.

We thundered down the beach. Maximus was completely stretched out into a racehorse run, and I felt as if I was flying.

It was just the two of us, the roar of the ocean, and the squeal of seagulls taking to the air as we barreled toward them. After about half a mile, I slowed Maximus to a walk, looking back to see Kam and Lori catching up to us at a leisurely canter. I suddenly remembered that crazy riding instructor in Washington State who had made me ride dressage patterns on a beach. All I could think was, *Wow, if she could only see me now! Now, this is riding!*

Kam had a big grin on his face too. It just warmed my heart to see him. He was now an oddly experienced horseperson, having boldly accepted every invitation to ride, crossed streams, jumped logs, loaded and unloaded horses from trailers, and even become skilled at backing up our own bumper-pulled trailer. I've always believed that husbands and wives have an opportunity to change each other for the positive. In many ways, Kam had always been the wind beneath my wings. We had certainly flown many places together, and he had always been the primary breadwinner, supporting me every step of the way. But I think, in some ways, my own crazy and seemingly endless love for horses had added something special to his life. His affection and admiration for these most noble creatures had also become a part of him.

After spending an hour riding at the beach, we had just turned back when we noticed Lori's buckskin horse was suddenly lame and limping badly. "What do you think is wrong with him, Lori?" Kam asked, concerned. Still mounted on the limping horse, he was now leaning over, trying to see the buckskin's feet.

"The horse has navicular," she replied.

"What's navicular?"

"It's an inflammation of the navicular bone. It causes pain in the heel, usually in both fronts."

"Does this happen often?"

"Yeah. For the last year, he's been lame a lot. We've been trying some corrective shoeing on him, but he seems to go lame every six weeks when his hooves start to grow out. He also goes lame sometimes if you canter him or go up and down steep hills."

"But we only cantered him a short distance, and that was on flat sand," Kam noted.

"I know," replied Lori. "It's a shame, because the horse is really well trained. We used to use him in team roping events and I've worked cattle on him all day long, but right now, we can't use him very much because, as you can see, we can't count on him."

As Kam and Lori talked, I looked at the horse's feet for the first time. Even though I'm no expert, for such a big quarter horse, his feet did look a little small to me, and they were narrow and upright, like little goat's feet. Kam decided to get off the horse and hand-walk him back to the trailer, as he didn't need any extra weight on his back.

The next day when I went back to Lori's to visit Maximus, I could see the buckskin was still hurting, and I felt bad for him. I decided to take him out of his pen and walk him over to a patch of grass as a treat. He limped as he walked, but the horse seemed to appreciate the treat nevertheless. As I stood beside him, letting him graze, I couldn't help admiring the horse's coloring. He had a lovely, golden coat, a dark-brown mane and tail, and a big white blaze down the front of his face. The white on his face was well matched with four white socks that ran from his feet to just below his knees. If you looked at him from the side, his white socks were so even, you'd swear this golden horse had been dipped in a bucket of white paint when he was a foal. Given his training and coloring, I was sure Lori could have sold him for a pretty penny if it wasn't for his lameness issues.

After about ten minutes of grazing, Maximus started whinnying, upset that I had taken the buckskin away from him. I watched the buckskin happily gobbling away and said, "So, I guess you and Maximus are good buddies now?"

Over the next few weeks, I could see that the buckskin was basically left in his pen most of the time, as Lori had plenty of young horses she was training and good, sound ranch horses to use at team roping events. With the buckskin being in the pen right beside Maximus, it was hard to ignore him. He was always staring at Kam and me, hoping for attention, and relishing the extra carrots we never forgot to bring him. Truly, the horse had the personality of a Saint Bernard, and Kam wanted to help him, so he started to read up on navicular.

One day, Kam and I were grooming Maximus when Kam walked over to pet the buckskin. Just as I was putting Maximus back in his pen, Kam looked at me and said, "Let's buy him from Lori."

"You want to buy the buckskin? You realize, hon, that he may only be able to walk—are you going to be OK with that? I mean, if his navicular gets real bad, we may not even be able to ride him, and he might end up costing a lot in vet bills."

"Yeah, I know," Kam replied, still petting the horse. Just at that moment, the buckskin lifted his head over the top fence rail and placed it on Kam's shoulder, nudging him gently.

"Oh, goodness," I said with a grin. "You're a goner now, aren't you?"

It was as if the horse was saying, "I'll be a good boy, I promise. Buy me, please! Pretty please?" The horse's pecan-colored eyes were looking lovingly into Kam's, and I knew the deal was done. Within a few days, we were the proud owners of a completely lame and limping quarter horse. We named him Montana.

The first thing we did after purchasing the horse was pull his shoes off. It was a difficult decision, but the corrective shoeing wasn't really working. Heck, the horse was still going lame, and we wanted to see if we could at least get him to the point where he could walk on his own four feet, pain-free. The first few weeks were the hardest to watch. Montana was incredibly sore, tiptoeing everywhere. It pained me to see him so uncomfortable, and at times, I questioned whether we were doing the right thing. But we stuck to plan. Kam purchased all kinds of hoof supplements, and we started the horse on a regimen of hyaluronic acid to lubricate his joints. In a few short weeks and after much research, Kam had gained a pretty good understanding of the various therapies for horses with navicular. Always one to seek natural remedies first, he took the horse off of the alfalfa cubes he was being fed and substituted them with lower-protein hay. We learned that mature horses actually have low protein needs and many do better on a low-protein, high-carbohydrate diet. Working with a "natural-hoof" farrier, we began to slowly change the shape of the horse's feet. Montana had what we were told were really contracted heels, and it was important to widen that area and improve the blood flow. Over the next six months, Kam and I spent hours hand-walking the horse up and down the sandy hill that ran from Lori's house down to the riding ring at the far back of the property. When the horse seemed more comfortable, we started walking him up and back Lori's long, gravel driveway, trying to toughen up his hooves and make them harder.

During this period, Montana had time to adapt to Kam and me. At first, he wasn't accustomed to his ears or nostrils being cleaned, and I think, in general, the horse had never been quite so fussed over. I remember one particular day, after giving him a full bath, cleaning his ears and nostrils, and trimming his tail, I was bent down, painting his hooves with Hooflex when I suddenly glanced up at him. Montana looked at me as if to say, "You people are really neat freaks, aren't you? I guess I'm going to have to get used to this!"

It took eight months, but we were finally able to ride him without shoes at a walk. The shape of his feet had improved, and so had his circulation. Interesting enough, even though Kam and I were now both working full-time, once we had two sound horses to ride, we ended up trail riding more than we ever had. As renters, we had ditched all forms of yard work and, not having stalls to clean or pastures to mow, we felt surprisingly chore-free, with plenty of time to ride on weeknights and weekends. We rode Maximus and Montana, now referred to as "the boys," along city streets and through neighborhoods, on trails around the golf course, and on the beach. All four of us were content to stay at a walk, and Montana seemed happy as a lark, loving his new life as a trail horse, with no more calves to chase or cows to sort.

While we have yet to find anything that Montana is afraid of, we have discovered that Maximus is utterly terrified of the *baaa* sound that goats make. We discovered this when Lori penned some goats on her property and Maximus began to have a complete meltdown. To get him used to the goats, we strategically put them right beside his pen for a full month, but that didn't help, as he seemed to view their cries as utterly demonic. Sometimes I would ride Maximus in the ring, and if he heard a *baaa* even from a distance, he would stop dead and start trembling in panic as if to say, "Did you hear that demon? Oh, they are horrible creatures. Please make them stop!" Eventually, Lori moved the goats to her mother's house, and Maximus returned to his old self, his prayers having been answered.

And it took a year, but eventually, we were able to ride Montana at a trot and canter without the horse going lame. I'm pleased to add that the horse kept his part of the bargain, carrying my husband safely and without fuss in any direction.

There was one fundamental question, however, that still gnawed. Although California has its obvious charms, like a handsome Hollywood actor, it never felt like a suitable match. Perhaps it was the fact that we were now in our mid-forties, or maybe seeing the unpacked boxes in the garage had started to fray our nerves. Like sticks in a river, over the years, Kam and I had traveled wherever his jobs took us. And like those sticks, we had become waterlogged and tired of the never-ending, constant rush forward. For whatever reason, it seemed now was the time to pull ashore, drag ourselves out of the river with the horses in tow, and set up camp. The questions were: where was a good place to start a fire, and to what kind of tree would we tie the horses?

19

Finding My Stirrups in a Desert Wash

Sometimes the smallest things can make you sit up and take notice. The melanoma first appeared on my left hip. Within a few weeks, an innocent-looking round beauty mark had morphed into the shape of a Z. "Surgery has to be scheduled this week. You can't delay," counseled my family doctor as she stared ominously at the biopsy results. "This is pretty serious."

The mark was only the size of a five-cent piece; that night as I Googled for websites about melanoma, there did seem to be cause for alarm. It was strange to think that something so small had the capacity to kill me on rather short notice.

DAGNY MOFID

Removing the now-menacing discoloration from my pasty-white thigh was my highest priority. The doctor explained that my skin was likely rebelling after a childhood spent mostly outdoors with not a moment's thought given to sunscreen. And, I had to admit, thirteen years of daily dog walking without wearing a hat probably hadn't helped matters.

I'm still not quite sure, though, why the melanoma appeared on my hip. Skin cancer, apparently, has its own agenda. Thanks to the American health care system, the evil spot was removed within five days. Unfortunately, a few months later, two squamous cell carcinomas were discovered on my left arm. Five months after that, a small spot on my nose began to bleed on and off for weeks. What seemed like a pimple that wouldn't heal turned out to be basal cell carcinoma. Yes, in a period of eight months, my skin had offered up a smorgasbord of skin cancers. Thankfully, we selected a talented plastic surgeon to perform Mohs surgery on my nose. There is certainly nothing like a skilled carver to leave you picture-perfect—the scar is barely perceptible. Of course, the subject was far from perfect to begin with, but at least my face is no worse for the wear.

Naturally, during this period, I found myself thinking about death in general and mine in particular. I've always believed that the thought of your own demise is actually good for you. I even read once that meditating on death is a recommended practice among Tibetan Buddhists. It helps eliminate one's fear of death, prepares one for a good rebirth, and reminds the person meditating how important it is to make life meaningful and appreciate every sacred breath. Now, I'm not perfectly convinced about the rebirth part, but the general notion seems reasonable. Although, *if* rebirth is possible, I'd like to put in a request to look more like Angelina Jolie, to be granted a scientific mind (or at least one that can understand calculus), and to come out of the womb screaming with confidence. Yes, even the mediocre can achieve when confident. But, in truth, I have no right to ask for anything additional. I was born to parents who loved me dearly, and I've been married to a man for almost thirty years who still likes to hold my hand. That is enough. And I'm happy to report that my skin seems to have settled back into its easy chair. Now the only things appearing regularly on my face are wrinkles. And, at least for the moment, my hips seem to be amusing themselves with dimples.

During this time of reflection, I became even more determined to find a place to settle down. I had developed a deep resentment toward moving boxes and wanted to find a home in which I could mount pictures and leave them up for at least thirty years. In my entire life, the longest period I had ever spent in any one house was six years. I realized that hoping for thirty years was a stretch, but one has to aim high. A friend once told me that each of us has a personal inner landscape—a landscape that you immediately connect with and want to spend time in. In my view, one can find beauty everywhere, even in the ugliest of places. In fact, when you live in an ugly place, it seems even more important to look for the beauty in it. But now I started to think about this notion of an inner landscape.

For some people, only the hum of a great city makes them feel alive. Cities are humanity's contribution to the world. It is in cities that we grow skyscrapers and museums, theaters and art galleries. These buildings are standing ovations to human culture. Crossing their thresholds, you are always invited to look up, pause for a moment, and admire human capability and creativity. In cities, restaurants and retail stores sprout like weeds and, once established, can sometimes survive for decades and even centuries. Like moths, we humans have always gravitated to the light and excitement of cities. Pulsating neon and digital screens now bathe our skylines, adding a particularly human rainbow of color and energy to the world.

For others, the tug of the ocean is strong. Sailing types enjoy the freedom to push out to sea, temporarily cutting ties to the solidity of earth for the swell and excitement of the ever-shifting ocean. They dare to look to the horizon and night sky for guidance. The ocean seems the very antithesis of land until you dive deep, where there too, you will find great mountain ranges, cliffs, and caves. I've always enjoyed leaning over the side of a boat and letting the rush of water pass through my fingers. Water seems like the very softest element, caressing one's palms without the slightest scratch. Yet, like words, the ocean can easily rise up and destroy with a vengeance. But not everyone needs to be on or in the water to enjoy it. For some, simply listening to ocean waves reminds them they are alive. The smell of the sea delights their senses. And like the pelicans and cormorants that soar past them, people walking on a beach feel free, even taking off their shoes to enjoy the moist sand under their bare feet.

Mountains pull adventurers to their peaks. For some, the physical challenge of a climb makes the views all the more rewarding. For other people, hikes through forests and along mountain trails provide a sort of walking meditation. The quiet allows them to decompress, and their minds, distracted only by the beauty of wildflowers or the simple scurry of a chipmunk, begin to settle. Soon they find themselves tuned in to the life around them, listening to variations in bird songs or stopping for a moment to watch a woodpecker plan for the future. Nature's skyscrapers certainly rival anything man can build. I, personally, feel like I've won a lottery when I get to see a wild animal where it needs to be—not in a zoo or in a cage, but free to live its own destiny. During a recent trip to Glacier National Park, Kam and I were gifted with the glimpse of a young grizzly bear eating berries on a mountainside. The next day, we came across a large bull moose resting in a glacial stream, letting the cool water refresh him on a hot afternoon. These are moments that take your breath away.

Given we grew up in Central Canada, Kam and I are quite comfortable hiking through boreal forests and canoeing on pristine lakes. We know the call of a loon, the sound of a beaver scurrying into the water, and the smell of a thick layer of pine needles. So it was a complete surprise to us when we fell head over heels in love with the desert. Like many life-changing experiences, it all happened on a whim.

Many years ago, I happened to pick up a horse magazine featuring an article about trail riding in southern Utah. The pictures were so dramatic. One photo I just couldn't get out of my mind. It was a picture of a string of horses following a mounted guide down a narrow path. The horses were descending carefully into a great chasm in the earth with a backdrop of unusual, orange-colored hoodoos. The picture was taken in Bryce Canyon National Park, and I was determined to get there one day. A few years later, Kam and I were thinking of going on a hiking trip with friends, and I suggested southern Utah, remembering that same photo.

Like seeing the Grand Canyon, one never forgets the first time you peer into Bryce Canyon. The entrance to the park is unassuming and looks like any other forest in southern Utah. Stands of fir, pine, aspen, and juniper trees are interspersed with small meadows and sagebrush. This is technically high desert country, and as we made our approach to the park, I couldn't help thinking, *Hmmm...nothing that special yet*. In fact, even as we stood on the back deck of the main park lodge, all we could see was a swath of trees in front of us. I kept thinking, *Goodness, where is this canyon*? Surprisingly, until you are virtually fifty feet from the edge of the Bryce amphitheater, you have no sense of the magnificence that awaits you. But then you get there and finally peer down into the giant, craterlike canyon filled with fantastical hoodoos that look like castles. The whole place is simply magical and looks like something from a fairy tale.

After a few days of hiking in this otherworldly landscape, we then set our sights on Zion National Park, which is only a short drive away. Zion is completely different from Bryce. When hiking in Bryce, you hike down into the canyon, but Zion rises up from the earth. Here, massive sandstone cliffs soar thousands of feet above you. The cliffs vary in color from cream, pink, and red and form an impressive backdrop to the unassuming Virgin River that has played a huge part in carving Zion. The park's microclimates allow a wide variety of plants to grow. On the same hike, one can see ferns growing below shaded water seeps and pass opuntia cacti basking in warm sunshine. The hikes we enjoyed in both parks left us exhausted, exhilarated, and apparently delirious. I'm not sure if we were blinded by the strong sunshine or just drunk on the nectar of agave, but we decided, then and there, to move to southern Utah. There were no "ifs" or "buts" to consider. We had found home.

Within six months, we bought an adobe-style house and settled in to the red desert of Saint George, Utah. Saint George is a small town of approximately 77,000 people. With over three hundred days of sunshine a year and no snow to worry about, Saint George is known as an active retirement mecca. I once even overheard a local joke that there are so many seniors there that they call it "God's waiting room."

Located two hours north of Las Vegas and four hours south of Salt Lake City, the city boasts a unique geography. The Saint George area is where the Colorado Plateau, Great Basin, and Mojave Desert converge. One suspects at some point in history, this area was a bubbling cauldron of geological activity. The land around town lifts up in so many directions, it is really hard to know just what to make of it. For example, the area near the local airport looks like the planet Mars. Kam always jokes that NASA's Mars rover is hidden just to the side of the airport road. Downtown Saint George looks like any town in New England except for a rather impressive backdrop of enormous, red sandstone cliffs. In the distance, one can see Pine Valley's Signal Peak. The summit is just over ten thousand feet and often snowcapped in the winter. To the northwest of the city, you will find Snow Canyon State Park, dominated by red, orange, and gray sandstone cliffs and punctuated by black lava rock.

"Imagine that," I said to Kam. "Black lava in a desert!" We had no idea where the lava had come from until we happened across the Cinder Cone Trail that took us to the very edge of a small, dormant volcano. While many might look at the same cliffs and mesas around town and find them too austere, for Kam and me, the land is strikingly beautiful. Perhaps it is the very raw nature of the desert that so captivates us. We admire the resilience of the native plants and gasp in awe at the cactus flowers that burst to life from their spiny stems in the spring. We love sitting among these ancient rocks, especially when a quiet stillness permeates the air. I am reminded of how much time has passed on this remarkable, ever-turning planet and how fleeting and unimportant our own lives are in the grand scheme of things.

When we first moved to Utah, all our friends seemed concerned at our decision. "Aren't there a lot of Mormons in Utah?" they asked. Yes, it is true, approximately 60 percent of the town's population is Latter Day Saints (or LDS, as they like to refer to themselves). But it hasn't been that difficult to adapt. Mormons seem to be very family-oriented types. They abstain from liquor and even coffee. I'm not quite sure why caffeine is banned, but even without morning java, they seem a rather industrious, hardworking lot. On Sundays, just like the Baptist churches of Texas, the local Mormon churches are packed. Mormon boys attend church in suits, and the girls attend in pretty dresses. On a regular basis, families gather at the local airport to welcome a friend or relative returning home from a "mission." They gather with smiles, balloons, and streamers and make even passers-by like me smile. So the result of all this is we have to live in a town that is well run and has a low crime rate and is filled with polite people. This is very difficult, as you can imagine.

How a girl from Montreal, Quebec ended up in southern Utah is still a bit of a mystery to me. Oddly enough, I feel more grounded than I ever have. Like the red rock and sandstone cliffs that surround Saint George, there is finally a sense of place in my heart and a sense of belonging. Perhaps there is something to be said for finding one's inner landscape. Ironically, the myriad turns in my life have taught me how important it is to slow down. I now want to be more the turtle than the hare. When you run too fast, life really does seem to blur. There is so much beauty in this world, I want to take the time to see and experience it. But I'm not referring to adventure travel. I'm talking about the beauty in a friend's smile, the laughter in my mother's voice, the love in my husband's eyes. Even listening to the cascading whistles of a canyon wren has become oddly important to me. I've finally stopped bouncing around from place to place and have learned not to take life too seriously. I guess you could say I finally found my stirrups. Who knew they were in a desert wash?

Maximus and Montana are boarded at a barn just twenty minutes from our home with about twenty-five other horses. The two of them are the best of horse friends, and they share a large sand pasture. I often find them sleeping peacefully on their sides in the sun or standing quietly under their shade cover together. We now ride "the boys" through red rock canyons and sandy desert washes, through forests of pinyon pines, and along gently flowing rivers. We've learned to sidestep cacti and avoid the sharp edges of black lava rocks. The horses have wiped their noses on the feathery plumes of sand sagebrush and watched jackrabbits bounce across the trail. On weekends, I sometimes trail ride with girlfriends, riding Montana and ponying Maximus. Maximus is twenty-four now but still eager to enjoy the trails, so I never leave him behind. Some of my friends own skittish and dangerous horses, while others are too afraid to leave the comfort of the riding ring. I've certainly ridden in their stirrups.

In truth, I never became the rider I wanted to be. One would not look at me on board a horse and say, "There is a great talent." But I guess, according to my old trainer Tom, I'm doing some things right. As he always said, "If your horse goes in the direction you point him, at the speed you want him to go, and he stays calm and relaxed, then you know you are doing things right." Ride after ride, Maximus and Montana are solid. And just as you come to trust a husband who always picks you up on time, you come to trust horses that, day after day, react as expected.

Now, one should never be lulled to the dangers of riding. My horses are not perfect, and I'm sure if a giant tree crashed to the ground beside us or if a snake bit one of their legs, I still might be unceremoniously ditched. Like wearing a seatbelt in a car, I'm never on board a horse without a helmet. Safety is always a priority. Fortunately, our horses' calm demeanors have finally soothed my jittery rider nerves. There are no more butterflies fluttering in the pit of my stomach. Imagined disasters are not racing through my mind. Stepping into the stirrup and swinging my leg into the saddle is akin to coming home. I suppose confident riders give a horse confidence, but for me, it was the other way around. My steady steeds built *my* confidence. It is truly important to ride the right horse for you. So, for all you timid, nervous riders out there, might I recommend Grandma-safe, "babysitter" horses over the age of fifteen? And when you find one, never let go—like good husbands, they are gems. For the nonriders among you, the next time you get close to a horse, if the owner allows it, take the time to pet its strong neck or gently stroke its forehead. Or, when driving past a field of horses, pull off the road, turn off the ignition, and take a moment to watch them playing or grazing in a pasture. Horses are magnificent creatures, and no time spent in their company is wasted. In fact, you might realize, as we have, that they have an odd capacity for soothing the soul.

Maximus and Montana are "keepers," and I will have them for as long as life lends them to me. I've decided that when they pass away, I will shed tears but not be sad. We four have galloped alongside ocean waves, trotted many trails, giggled as quail crossed our paths, and enjoyed quiet lunches together on the side of a trail. After tying the horses to the low branches of a mesquite tree, we always pull carrots out of our saddlebags. The horses begin licking their lips as soon as we unzip the bags, knowing their treats are on the way. Yes, we all have much to be thankful for. We know the smell of eucalyptus and the smell of creosote after a desert rain. We've watched mourning doves whiz past us at torpedolike speeds and listened to the solitary caw of a black crow break the deafening silence of a canyon. Our horses have looked eagerly around every curve and contentedly at the trailer that takes them safely home.

As you can see, the horses have lived and live well, and one day when I'm an old lady, weak and bedridden, I'll close my eyes and hear the thundering hooves and remember Maximus and Montana's soft noses, their warm, strong necks and their ever-turning, fuzzy ears. And I will laugh, remembering my crazy Merlot throwing orange construction pylons in the air like a juggler. I'm sure I'll be very wrinkled from years spent outdoors, and my body may show no sign of its former strength, but I'll bet that when the doctor bends over my bed to look into my eyes, he will see a twinkle, and on a closer look, he just might see horses dancing in them.

The End

Made in the USA
San Bernardino, CA
16 March 2015